Macdonald Insiders

Oil Rig

Neil Potter

Macdonald Educational

Series Editor Philippa Stewart
Edited by Caroline Russum
Design Peter Benoist
Production Philip Hughes
Picture Research Sue Bonney
                  Jenny de Gex

Macdonald & Co (Publishers) Ltd
Maxwell House
Worship Street
London EC2A 2EN

ISBN 0 356 05584 1

Printed by New Interlitho
Milan, Italy

First published 1977
Reprinted 1982
© Macdonald Educational 1977

Oil Rig

Contents

Oil today

They are a strange, restless crowd, these people who roam the world in search of oil. They can be found in the remote jungles of Indonesia or in the rain forests of the Amazon; in the biting cold of the Arctic or the steaming swamps of Nigeria. They battle against the vicious winds and high seas off Australia or Britain. They are at work in the hurricane-swept South China Sea and the Gulf of Mexico; in the near-empty burning desert sands of the Middle East or the sunlit waters of the Mediterranean Sea. Looking for oil is a truly international business.

But why is this "liquid gold" so important? It is as old as time itself. Noah is said to have smeared the Ark with two coats of bitumen, collected from oil which had seeped to the surface of the earth. Thousands of years ago the Chinese were using oil as fuel to light their lamps.

Today oil is part of our way of life. Oil is energy. It is fuel, for lorries, ships and aircraft, for power stations, for factories and for heating. It can be turned into fertilizers, into nylon and into plastics. Today oil provides 42 per cent of the world's energy, with coal providing 30 per cent, natural gas 20 per cent, and nuclear and hydroelectric power 8 per cent.

Today, for a number of reasons, less oil is being used than in recent years. In 1981, throughout the world, 2,890.3 million tonnes (59.1 million barrels a day) of crude oil were produced, a decrease of 6.2 per cent on 1980. This was due to the world economic recession, conservation, and the use of other energy resources. More and more countries are taking control of their own production, especially in the Middle East. Many of these producing countries have joined together to form the Organization of Petroleum Exporting Countries (OPEC) to protect their interests.

But the supply of oil will not last for ever. Like coal, oil is a fossil fuel, formed in the earth over millions of years. Once it has been taken out of the ground, it can never be replaced. World reserves of oil total 92.1 thousand million tonnes, with 53.5 per cent of that in the Middle East.

But the search for new oilfields continues. In the early days it was the small independent groups who looked for oil; today it is big business. There are many national and international companies, the biggest of which are known as "The Seven Sisters". These are British Petroleum, Royal Dutch Shell, and the American companies, Exxon, Mobil, Texaco, Gulf and Standard Oil of California. These are, so to speak, the "generals". In the front line are the "troops": the drilling contractors, supply companies, helicopter pilots, divers, technicians and geologists whose work we look at in this book.

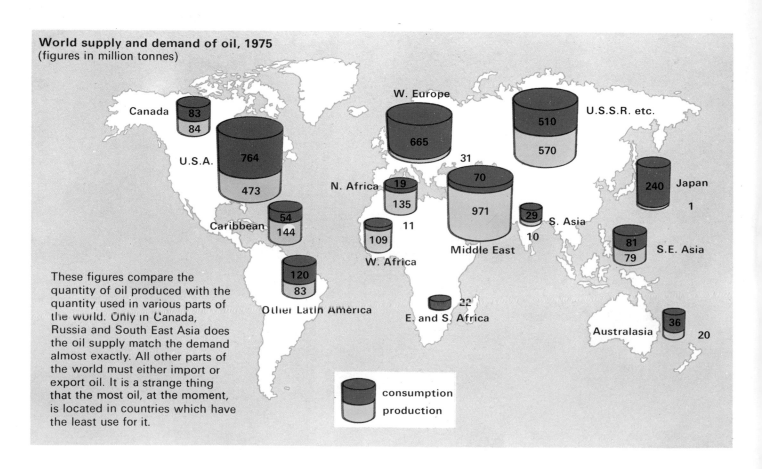

World supply and demand of oil, 1975
(figures in million tonnes)

These figures compare the quantity of oil produced with the quantity used in various parts of the world. Only in Canada, Russia and South East Asia does the oil supply match the demand almost exactly. All other parts of the world must either import or export oil. It is a strange thing that the most oil, at the moment, is located in countries which have the least use for it.

Canada 83 / 84
U.S.A. 764 / 473
Caribbean 54 / 144
Other Latin America 120 / 83
W. Europe 665
U.S.S.R. etc. 510 / 570
N. Africa 19 / 135
W. Africa 11 / 109
Middle East 70 / 971
31
S. Asia 29 / 10
Japan 240 / 1
S.E. Asia 81 / 79
E. and S. Africa 22
Australasia 36 / 20

consumption
production

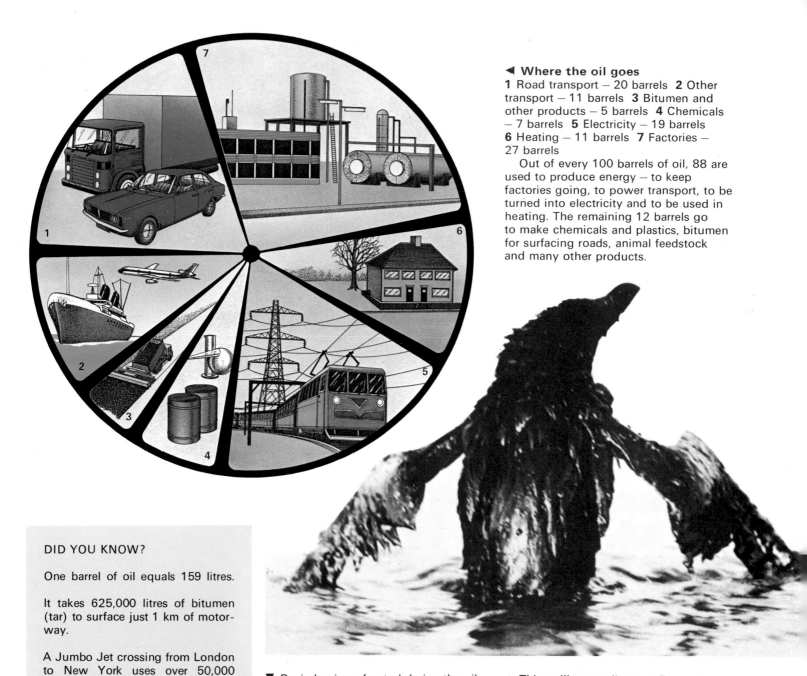

◄ Where the oil goes
1 Road transport — 20 barrels **2** Other transport — 11 barrels **3** Bitumen and other products — 5 barrels **4** Chemicals — 7 barrels **5** Electricity — 19 barrels **6** Heating — 11 barrels **7** Factories — 27 barrels

Out of every 100 barrels of oil, 88 are used to produce energy — to keep factories going, to power transport, to be turned into electricity and to be used in heating. The remaining 12 barrels go to make chemicals and plastics, bitumen for surfacing roads, animal feedstock and many other products.

DID YOU KNOW?

One barrel of oil equals 159 litres.

It takes 625,000 litres of bitumen (tar) to surface just 1 km of motorway.

A Jumbo Jet crossing from London to New York uses over 50,000 litres of aviation kerosine.

Oil accounts for half the cargo carried each year by all ships.

▼ Panic buying of petrol during the oil crisis in 1973. At this time the oil producers belonging to OPEC decided they should reduce oil exports to conserve their resources. Within months oil prices quadrupled.

▲ This guillemot will never fly again. It has been caught up in an oil slick after a tanker has gone aground. As more and more oil is transported around the world, pollution becomes an increasing problem.

Looking for oil

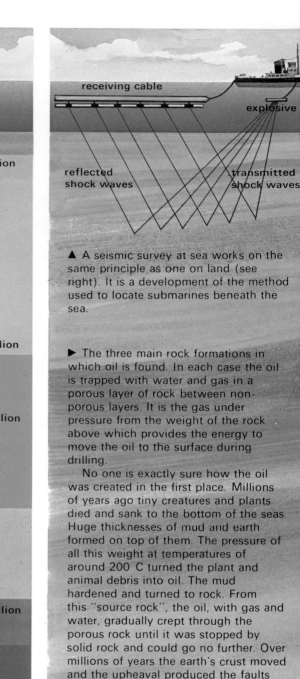

"If you want to shoot a bear, you figure out from all the information you can get where a bear is likely to be and then go and look for one. If you want to find an oilfield you figure out from all the information where it is possible for an oilfield to be. Then you go there and look for it". That is how one geologist described how to set about finding oil.

The decision to go and look is based on a study of known facts about an area. Then aerial photographs are taken. One camera shot taken from a height of about 8,000 metres will cover 500 sq km. In a few hours an area of 2,500 sq km can be photographed. That can save a great deal of trekking through jungle or desert.

From the aerial photographs the geologist will choose suitable spots for examining the rocks below the surface in greater detail. Each rock has a history, a changing character. The geologist looks for clues, like a detective, to tell him more about them. He cannot actually go down and have a look. So "seeing eyes" have been developed, instruments providing information which the geologist can study in the laboratory.

The fieldwork is done by a survey team, usually made up of a geologist, a geophysicist and their helpers. They use many instruments; one is a gravitimeter, which measures the differences of gravity between points on the earth's surface. They measure the direction and intensity of the earth's magnetic field with magnetometers. They carry out seismic surveys to investigate the depth and character of the rocks.

But there is still only one way to know if there is oil down there . . . to drill a hole. At various stages of drilling, the geologist asks for core samples to be brought up. These are cylindrical sections of the rock strata which provide him with much information. Throughout the drilling, "mud" (not just ordinary mud but a carefully prepared chemical compound) is pumped down the hollow drill pipe and comes out at the bottom through holes in the drill bit. It is about as thick as pea soup. It cools the bit and controls the pressure. It also brings back to the surface pieces of rock and organic matter. These cuttings are carefully examined and tested for oil traces.

When oil is found, the well may be plugged with concrete while a decision is made as to whether to produce from it. But of course the oilmen do not always strike lucky. Around the world some 11,000 exploration holes are drilled every year. Only one in 20 will show oil. In 1981, it cost something like £45,000 a day to hire and operate an offshore drilling rig. Looking for oil is expensive.

▲ A seismic survey at sea works on the same principle as one on land (see right). It is a development of the method used to locate submarines beneath the sea.

▶ The three main rock formations in which oil is found. In each case the oil is trapped with water and gas in a porous layer of rock between non-porous layers. It is the gas under pressure from the weight of the rock above which provides the energy to move the oil to the surface during drilling.

No one is exactly sure how the oil was created in the first place. Millions of years ago tiny creatures and plants died and sank to the bottom of the seas. Huge thicknesses of mud and earth formed on top of them. The pressure of all this weight at temperatures of around 200 C turned the plant and animal debris into oil. The mud hardened and turned to rock. From this "source rock", the oil, with gas and water, gradually crept through the porous rock until it was stopped by solid rock and could go no further. Over millions of years the earth's crust moved and the upheaval produced the faults and anticlines in which the oil has collected.

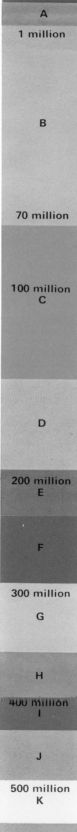

◀ A geological time scale
The figures indicate the number of years. Geologists must be completely familiar with these periods and the fossils that are characteristic of them.

A Quaternary
B Tertiary
C Cretaceous
D Jurassic
E Triassic
F Permian
G Carboniferous
H Devonian
I Silurian
J Ordovician
K Cambrian
L Pre-Cambrian

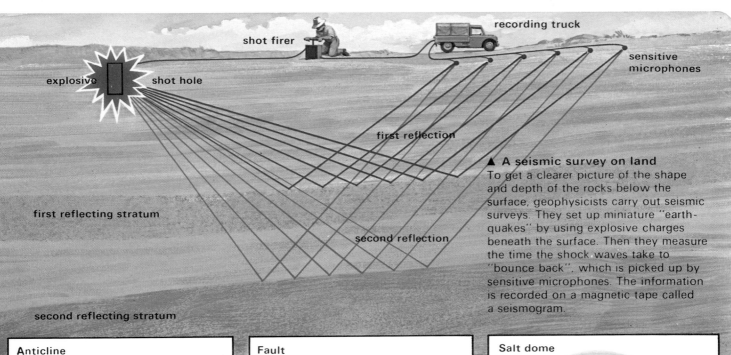

shot firer

recording truck

explosive   shot hole

sensitive microphones

first reflection

first reflecting stratum

second reflection

second reflecting stratum

▲ **A seismic survey on land**
To get a clearer picture of the shape and depth of the rocks below the surface, geophysicists carry out seismic surveys. They set up miniature "earth-quakes" by using explosive charges beneath the surface. Then they measure the time the shock waves take to "bounce back", which is picked up by sensitive microphones. The information is recorded on a magnetic tape called a seismogram.

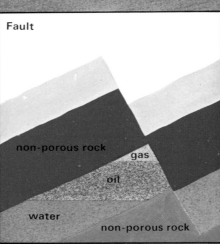

Anticline

non-porous rock

gas

oil

non-porous rock

water

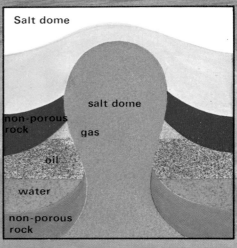

Fault

non-porous rock

gas

oil

water

non-porous rock

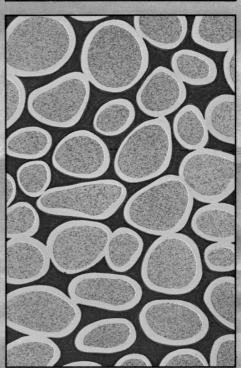

Salt dome

non-porous rock

salt dome

gas

oil

water

non-porous rock

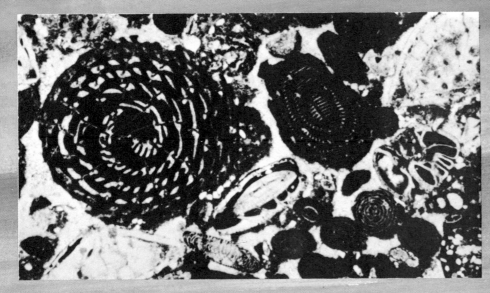

▲ A piece of rock magnified 100 times under a microscope. Geologists can obtain much information about the rock by identifying the fossils which are found in it.

▶ The diagram shows that oil is not found in great pools or lakes but lies trapped in the tiny spaces between the grains of sand (orange) in porous rock. Water (blue) is also trapped in the pores.

Geologists at work

Geologists and geophysicists play a vital role in the search for oil. On them rests the task of recommending where the "wildcat" well is to be drilled and advising on the course of the operation. The geologist will do much of the fieldwork, examining the physical aspects of an area and making a detailed study of the rocks found there. The geophysicist is responsible for the more technical side, taking the seismic and gravimetric surveys which will help to assess the likelihood of striking oil.

A different world

The young geologist, armed with his degree, coming straight from university, will find conditions in the oil industry very different from the calm and quiet of the laboratory. His "classroom" now may be in swampy forests, in the bitter cold of the Arctic, in the burning desert or on a drillship or rig 500 km out in a stormy ocean. His laboratory may be a mobile caravan or a cramped corner on an off-shore rig.

He has much to learn. The exact location of a rig to drill a "wildcat" (exploratory well) in an unknown region will be fixed on a detailed map of the area by a conference of experienced geologists and geophysicists. They will have assessed and debated all the information received. The position will then be checked with the drilling superintendent and other specialists, as there are many factors to be considered. The drilling of a well calls for teamwork between the drilling crew and the geologist on the spot. It is essential that the geologist understands the language of the drillers and the simple principles of drilling. He should know the rig, names of important parts and how they work. He should understand the problems of drilling. He must know about cuttings, which the drilling mud brings up, how to study them, how to learn from them what is happening down the hole. He must know how cores, the cylindrical samples of rock which are specially drilled, are obtained and when exactly to drill for them. He must be able to build up a "picture" of the various layers of rock below the ground.

▼ A seismic team at work in the mangrove swamps of Nigeria. The geologist is studying a seismogram.

▲ A geologist examining rock samples to determine their fossil content.

Work in the tropics

For some years oil companies have been interested in the tropical island of Timor, off Australia. Two young geologists, using rough geographical maps prepared some years before, were sent out. Each was given an area of 1,300 sq km to work. Equipment consisted of a land-rover each, four native helpers, camping equipment, dry food and supplies to last for at least three months at a time. Their base camp was 110 km away, so each day a radio call was maintained. If supplies were short, a land-rover was sent out. Vegetables, fruit and rice were bought locally.

Timor is divided in half by a 3,000-metre mountain range. It has, in the southern half, two wet seasons and one long dry season lasting five months. The search for oil was concentrated mainly in the river bed areas. During the second wet season conditions here could be very treacherous. After only an hour's rain up in the mountains, a previously dry river would become a raging torrent, cutting the geologists off from their base camp.

A normal day for the geologists began at 4.30 a.m. They started work at 6 a.m., working on their surveys within one day's walking distance of the camp, which was moved each month. They took a long

▲ Field work can be lonely but challenging. To the geologist this empty landscape in Iran offers the exciting possibility of discovering oil-bearing rock.

▶ Rock cuttings, taken from the drilling mud, are washed before they can be studied under the microscope.

---

lunch, simply because the heat (36°C on average) and the high level of humidity made work unbearable during the mid-day period. The main pests were mosquitoes and ants, and because of the dangers of malaria in the rain forests an anti-malaria tablet had to be taken each day.

One important aspect of the work was a knowledge of the local native language, plus Portuguese, so they could negotiate with the market people, and with the local headman for permission to carry out the search.

For Europeans the main source of danger was snakes, and strangely enough, water buffalo. On one occasion the three native helpers, and one of the white geologists, were surveying a dried up river bed, when out of the bush came a charging buffalo. The natives are veget-

arians. The white man, being a meat eater, had a repugnant smell to the buffalo and so he was the target. There was only one thing to do . . . head for the nearest tree, and fortunately there were plenty of them. The native helpers simply stood there laughing.

A special breed

The previous account is just one illustration of the kinds of conditions geologists have to work under. The search for oil is international. Within weeks of completing a survey in the jungle, the same geologists might be flying to the Arctic or the desert, where the work will be the same, but the conditions, to put it mildly, rather different. It is lonely, hard work. It is not for nothing that geologists have been called "the unsung heroes of the oil business".

Work on a seismic party in the desert, for example, is a fulltime job, 10 to 16 hours a day, seven days a week. Usually a skilled technician will work three weeks on and then be given a week off although schedules vary. In some cases, where there have been no back-up personnel to relieve workers, key personnel have worked straight through for as long as a year. This can be dangerous, mentally and physically, unless the person has such a work load that he does not become bored. If he cannot keep himself occupied, he will become irritable and quick-tempered. When he reaches such a state of mind it is better for morale to allow him time off, regardless of whether there is a relief or not.

"To live and work on a seismic party anywhere takes a special breed — a person with a high sense of adventure, dedication to his work, a willingness to work long hours for low pay, pride in doing a job well, the ability to pack up and move on at a moment's notice and to be self-disciplined. This type of person is slowly vanishing from the scene." This is how one American geologist summed up the operation.

Qualifications and pay

Geologists must have an honours degree in geology. Geophysicists have to have a thorough knowledge of the principles of gravity, and know how to acquire and interpret aeromagnetic and seismic data. They will usually have a degree in geology, or physics, with subsidiary in geology.

The pay that a geologist or geophysicist will earn varies from company to company. But the starting salary for a graduate will probably be about £8,500. If he has a PhD he will get £9,500. Senior geologists with a minimum of ten years experience and responsible for a large area will get anything over £22,000 plus allowances. If work is done overseas there are other allowances and tax benefits.

derrick

travelling block

flexible hose

kelly

rotary table

pipe rack

drawworks

mud pumps

mud tank

power unit

blow-out preventer

casing

drill pipe

drill bit

A rotary drilling rig
The principles behind the drilling process are the same whether the rig is on land or at sea. This diagram illustrates the main parts of a rig, many of which will be described in greater detail on pages 16 and 17. The basic structure of the rig is the derrick. The drilling itself is done by a drill bit, made of very hard steel at the end of a drill string, which can be extended by adding extra lengths of pipe. The bit is rotated by the action of the kelly, a square section of pipe which is always the uppermost section of the drill string. Mud is circulated round the system to keep it cool.

Desert heat

The oil industry as we know it today was "born" in the Middle East in May 1908 when, after six years of exploration in the Zagreb Mountains, Iran, a jet of oil 15.2 metres high shot out of the top of the derrick. Oil was discovered in Iraq in 1927 and in 1938 it was located in Saudi Arabia. Today the belt of oilfields lying between Turkey and Oman produces more than one-third of the world's total output. Almost two-thirds of the world's known oil reserves are still there. So exploration continues in some of the most challenging areas in the world.

Conditions in the desert are not easy. The daily temperature in the shade can be 50°C in the summer and even at night it can be more than 40°C. The humidity can be so high in the morning that there is dense fog in the air, clinging to everything. During the hottest part of the day it is almost impossible to handle tools or touch metal. Yet in the winter temperatures approach freezing in some areas. Sandstorms can last a week. It is often impossible to see further than a few metres in front of your face. Protective eye goggles are issued to all workers.

The desert sand blows into the running gear of lorries and trucks. It gets into the moving parts of rigs. Special dust and humidity extractors are used to keep sand out of the electrical generators and motors. The driller's control panels are completely sealed in to protect them. The drilling camp itself may be a 12-hour drive from the base camp. Some supplies are flown in from the base, so light airstrips have to be built.

All the rig equipment is designed to be taken apart and loaded quickly and easily, as the rig has frequently to be moved to a new location. It is no easy task to move these 800-tonne rigs across the desert, by convoys of trucks. Sometimes the rig is lifted into the new position by helicopter. In flat areas it can be moved by truck as a complete unit.

In sand areas it is almost impossible for a normal vehicle to move without getting stuck. Vehicles are fitted with massive 3-metre diameter tyres, which spread the vehicle's load over a much greater area and provide a floating action over the sand.

Rules for travelling and operating in the desert are rigid. Drilling companies insist that every traveller must carry water with him and must check out with the radio operator before setting out. They must keep in touch. If a vehicle breaks down, the men must stay with it, for a vehicle is easier to spot from the air than a speck of a human being against the ocean of sandy desert. Lives have been lost for failure to observe this simple rule.

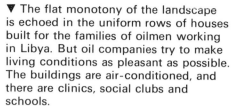

▼ The flat monotony of the landscape is echoed in the uniform rows of houses built for the families of oilmen working in Libya. But oil companies try to make living conditions as pleasant as possible. The buildings are air-conditioned, and there are clinics, social clubs and schools.

▲ Old meets new in Chad, Africa. Nomads brought their horses to drink here centuries before oil was found. In many desert areas, water is in short supply and wells have to be sunk for water used in the drilling process.

▼ A cloud of sand shoots up in the sky during a seismic explosion in Abu Dhabi. By measuring the time the shock waves take to "bounce back", geologists find out more about the rocks below the surface.

▲ Drilling operations in Oman. This worker is running casing into the drill hole. During the course of drilling the sides of the hole may crumble and cave in, so the drill string is removed and a steel casing cemented into place. Each time this is done, a smaller bit has to be used to fit inside the casing.

11

Lassoo that berg

The relentless search for oil goes on high up in the Arctic Circle, in Alaska, Canada and in the seas off Labrador. For generations the Eskimos, hunting for seals and whales, had seen oil seeping out of the ground. They used it to light their lamps. Now modern drillers are up there. Big fields like those at Prudhoe Bay on the North Slope of Alaska have been discovered. Some geologists say that there could be 25,000 million barrels of oil to be recovered from these Arctic wastes and frozen seas.

But finding the oil is no easy task. It requires hardy men, special equipment, and large sums of capital — largely because of the Arctic climate. For it is bitterly cold there. Temperatures drop to —45°C and there is a biting wind. The cold can numb the brain and sap a man's energy.

Men wear down-filled parkas, and down trousers over thick woollen underwear, Arctic boots, down mittens and, most essential of all, a face mask. According to one description, "They look more like the stereotype of polar explorers . . . than oilmen whose work involves hard muscle, quick reflexes and perspiration. Hindered by protective garb, the efficiency of a drilling crew is reduced to half that expected in California or Texas oilfields".

Men can work at —45°C, but machines cannot. Metal snaps like a twig. Engines have to be kept going 24 hours a day; eventually after running non-stop for about 18 months they wear out. Drilling decks have to be protected and specially hardened steel bits and pipe have to be used.

But it is a land of contrasts. When drilling crews first tried to work in the Arctic summer, short though it is, they found themselves bogged down in the soft, soggy tundra. So work was restricted to the winter months. During that time, however, drillers must work six weeks on, for 12 hours a day. Then they have two weeks' leave in civilization.

One of the problems of drilling in these regions is the permafrost, the first 600 metres below the surface which is a permanently frozen mixture of rock, gravel, silt and ice. A delicate relationship exists between the tundra and the permafrost. A break in the insulating cover of the tundra would allow the permafrost to thaw, causing erosion and disturbing the growth of vegetation.

So special drilling techniques have been developed. The rigs rest on gravel pads to protect the ground. Chilled diesel oil, which has a temperature well below freezing, is used in drilling the first 600 metres of the hole to prevent the permafrost from melting. Crude oil comes out of the well bores at the reservoir temperature of 70°C. The effect of this on the frozen ground could be disastrous so insulated casing is used to line the well sides.

▼ Heavy snow covers this drilling camp in Spitzbergen in the Arctic Ocean. Special equipment is needed to cope with the harsh weather conditions.

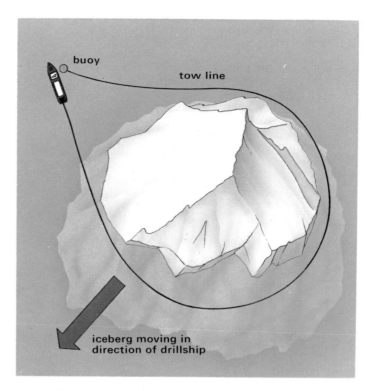

▲ This native Eskimo is employed as a roustabout at an exploratory oil well in the Northwest Territories, Canada. He is well wrapped-up against the bitter cold. It is difficult to know whether he is on the night shift or whether it is simply the winter, when the sun sets in November and does not rise again until mid-January.

▲▼ Icebergs are a frequent hazard in the Arctic. A 24-hour watch is kept to ensure that none get too close to the drill-ship. If an iceberg is on a collision course a specially commissioned ship, on station 5 km from the drillship, lassoos it with a tow rope and pulls it out of the way. This ship can tow bergs weighing up to 100 million tonnes!

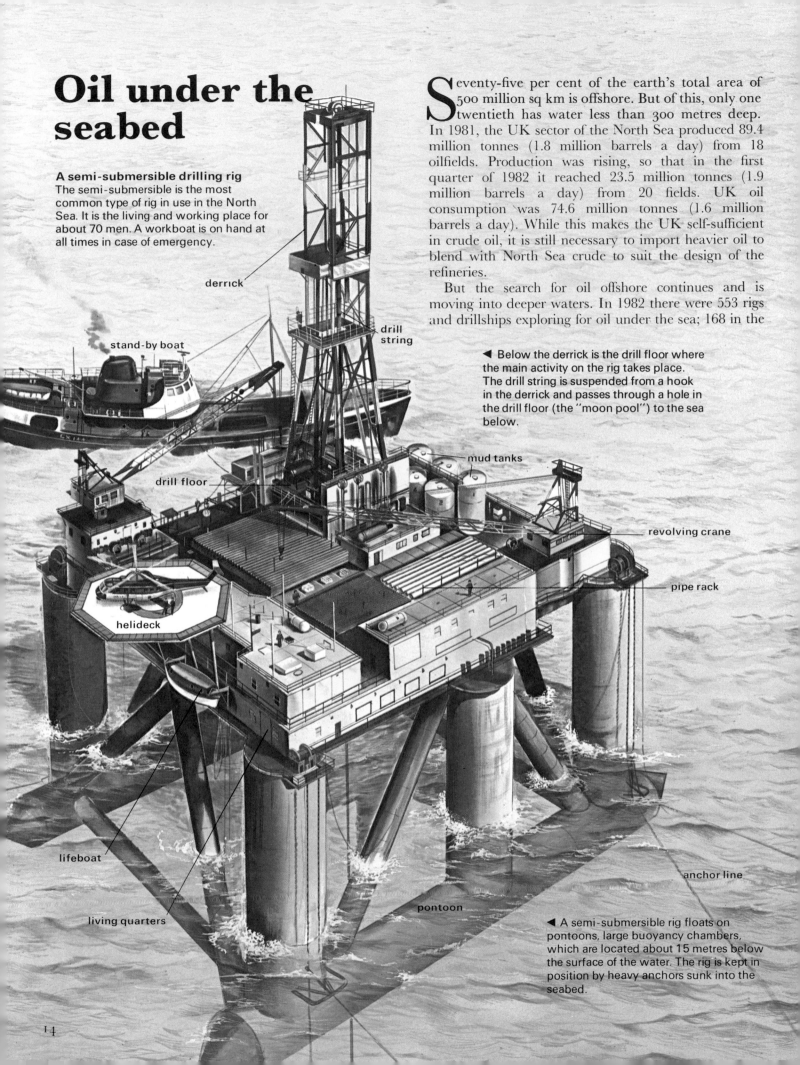

Oil under the seabed

A semi-submersible drilling rig
The semi-submersible is the most common type of rig in use in the North Sea. It is the living and working place for about 70 men. A workboat is on hand at all times in case of emergency.

Seventy-five per cent of the earth's total area of 500 million sq km is offshore. But of this, only one twentieth has water less than 300 metres deep. In 1981, the UK sector of the North Sea produced 89.4 million tonnes (1.8 million barrels a day) from 18 oilfields. Production was rising, so that in the first quarter of 1982 it reached 23.5 million tonnes (1.9 million barrels a day) from 20 fields. UK oil consumption was 74.6 million tonnes (1.6 million barrels a day). While this makes the UK self-sufficient in crude oil, it is still necessary to import heavier oil to blend with North Sea crude to suit the design of the refineries.

But the search for oil offshore continues and is moving into deeper waters. In 1982 there were 553 rigs and drillships exploring for oil under the sea; 168 in the

◄ Below the derrick is the drill floor where the main activity on the rig takes place. The drill string is suspended from a hook in the derrick and passes through a hole in the drill floor (the "moon pool") to the sea below.

derrick

drill string

stand-by boat

mud tanks

drill floor

revolving crane

pipe rack

helideck

lifeboat

living quarters

pontoon

anchor line

◄ A semi-submersible rig floats on pontoons, large buoyancy chambers, which are located about 15 metres below the surface of the water. The rig is kept in position by heavy anchors sunk into the seabed.

Gulf of Mexico; 62 off South America; 63 in the North Sea; 68 in the Middle East; 41 off Africa; 53 in south-east Asia; and 23 in the Mediterranean.

This search under the seabed did not just happen because an oilman said "Let's go to sea". It crept gradually from the onshore fields of California, Russia and Venezuela, into the shallow waters, just off the coasts. Then, as drilling equipment developed, it moved into deeper waters. Now a new world water depth record has been set by a drillship drilling in 1050 metres of water in the Andaman Sea, off Thailand.

The North Sea has been a "technical school" for offshore drilling. The lessons learned there have led to the breakthrough which has enabled the search to move into really deep waters. But it has been a hard school. On land the rig is always mobile. It can be taken to pieces and moved to a new site on a truck or by helicopter. Offshore the rig must be housed on a structure capable of floating on the water, and to move it has to be towed by tugs or travel under its own power. During the winter in the North Sea, 25-metre-high waves crash against the rig, hurricane force winds blow, and supply boats, bringing everything from food to drill pipe, have to operate in storms, often travelling more than 500 km from base.

Systems had to be developed to keep the floating rig properly aligned with a drill hole hundreds of metres below on the ocean floor. The well-head and pressure control systems have to be set on a stable base—the seabed. A reliable system for determining the position of the rig or ship in relation to the hole had to be devised.

Drillships have *dynamic positioning* by which a control computer on the bridge signals the propellers to move the ship forwards or backwards, and "thrusters" in the side of the hull to push it to one side or the other. A 6-metre square hole in the bottom of the ship's hull allows the drill string to reach the well hole from the work floor above. The drill system had to be devised so that it could be easily "slipped" in case the weather was too stormy for drilling.

But still the drillers are not satisfied. More and more refinements, improvements and new techniques are being developed all the time.

Production platforms

Once a drilling rig has struck oil and the decision has been taken to produce from the oilfield, then the production platform comes into operation. Unlike the drilling rig, which is designed to be moved from one place to another, the platform is a fixed structure, fastened to the seabed. Production platforms are made of steel or concrete, and are massive structures, much larger than drilling rigs. Most platforms can also be distinguished by their flare stack, which flares off excess gas. Work and conditions on board a production platform, however, are very similar to those on a rig.

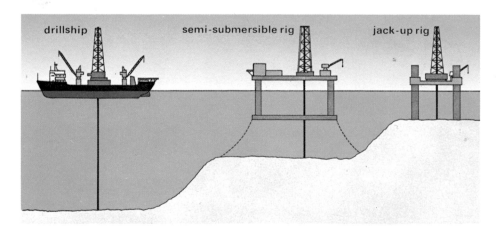

◀ Different types of drilling rigs

In shallow waters up to 100 metres deep the jack-up rig is used. This rig is towed to its destination, where its legs are attached to the seabed and its platform jacked-up to the required level above the sea.

The semi-submersible can operate in most conditions and in depths of 300 metres or more.

The drillship can operate in depths of up to 6 km deep because its dynamic positioning system keeps it in place without the need for anchors.

Drilling for oil

In the history of the oil industry it is sometimes said that the Egyptians building the Pyramids in 3000 BC used the rotary method to drill holes. By AD 1100 the Chinese were drilling to depths of 1,000 metres by this method with very primitive equipment. But modern well-drilling really began with Colonel Drake's well at Titusville in Pennsylvania in 1859. This first oil derrick was 10 metres high and drilled to a depth of 21 metres to produce 25 barrels a day.

Today a derrick is erected to about 40 metres high. Machinery is installed so that the drilling bit can be turned with a rotary movement. The drilling platform is the real working site of the group of men known as the "roughnecks". The round steel construction in its middle is the rotary table. It is driven by a special engine and it has to rotate the entire drill string. This is done by means of the "kelly". This is a 12-metre-long square or hexagonal pipe, attached to the top of the drill string and turned by the rotary table. It is used to transmit the twisting movement from the machinery to the drill pipe and so to the bit. Drill pipe is usually in lengths of about 10 metres and so, as the hole goes deeper and deeper, more and more lengths have to be added to the drill string.

Nearby is the drilling mud system, which cools and lubricates the drill bit and keeps the pressure down, and also carries rock cuttings to the surface. For deep drilling to 3,000 metres, several tonnes of chemicals will be used. The experienced man in charge of this operation is the mud engineer. By examining the mud in his laboratory he can give the driller details of how the drilling is progressing.

Coming from the slush pumps, the stand pipe and the rotary hose, the mud enters the swivel and from there it goes into the hollow shaft of the kelly, the drill string and down to the bottom of the hole.

There is no basic difference between an onshore and an offshore rig. They both do the same job—drill a hole. At sea it can take 90 days to sink a well 2.5 km into the seabed.

In the olden days onshore, an experienced driller could tell by the "feel" of the pipe how things were going. Nowadays it is a much more sophisticated operation. On the drill platform is the "dog house", where the driller operates. He is an experienced drilling engineer. In front of him he has a mass of dials, gauges and controls. These tell him everything he needs to know about volume, temperature, pump pressure and density of the mud. They tell him the rate of penetration of the hole, the bit weight, and speed of revolutions of the rotary table. There are controls for blow-out preventers and alarms for all emergencies.

▲ A derrickman at work high up on the "monkey board". He is guiding the new section of pipe being added to the drill string (right). At all times the derrickman must wear a safety chain known as a "belly buster".

Drill bits

The most important tool in the whole operation of drilling is the bit. It consists of a shaft and three or four rollers with longer or shorter teeth made of very hard steel. There are three types of teeth. Long ones are used for soft rock formations and short ones for hard formations. For extremely hard rock, special bits are used, studded with diamonds. The teeth break the rock cuttings loose from the bottom of the hole when the bit rolls around and the mud stream takes them up to the surface.

A bit usually lasts about 30 hours although diamond bits may last 100 hours or more. It takes some 15 hours of hard physical work to change a bit, as the whole of the drill string has to be pulled up.

1. drill pipe stem

2. hole

3. drill bit

4. mud returns up hole

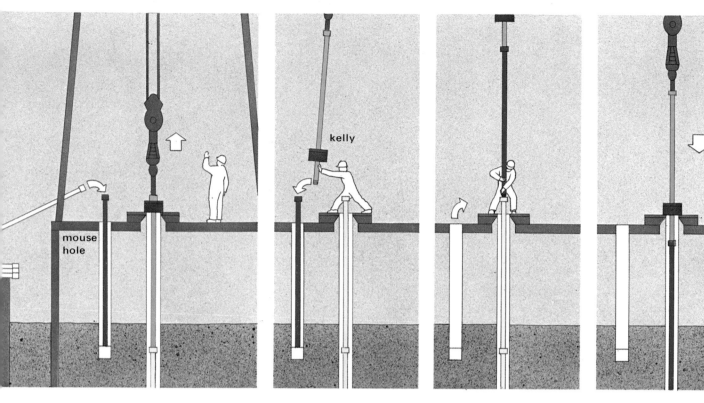

▲ Adding a length of drill pipe

The new length of drill pipe is run from the pipe rack into the "mouse hole". The drill string is hauled up and blocked by the slips in the rotary table. The kelly is screwed off and connected to the new pipe. The kelly and the new pipe are then hauled up high and connected with the rest of the drill string. The slips are withdrawn and drilling begins again.

▶ A team of roughnecks on the drill floor. It is hard, dirty and even dangerous work as the floor is permanently slippery from the mud and water. Great care must be taken to prevent accidents and teamwork is all-important.

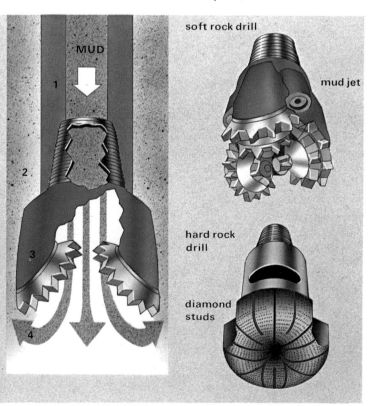

A drilling team

A drilling team is a highly disciplined, highly trained, physically fit group of men. They need to be. Most companies in the North Sea operate a four-crew shift system, based on 12 hours on, 12 hours off, either on a seven days on, seven days off, or 14 days on, 14 days off basis. So there are four workers for every position. It is hard, physical, dirty, even dangerous work. The vocabulary might sound romantic, like that of the old-style cowboys: "roughnecks", "roustabouts", "tool pushers", "the kelly", "the gooseneck". But drilling is a highly organized operation and the men who do it need to be tough.

▲ A tool pusher at the controls of a semi-submersible rig.

The drilling superintendent

All drilling is under the control of a drilling superintendent. He is usually based on shore and spends much of his time in administrative work, in planning, and in supervising. He will have a degree (usually in engineering) plus long years of field experience and in-company training. He is responsible for all the operations of the company in a given area. He will be employed on a contract and may earn more than £30,000 a year.

The drilling engineer

The next man in the chain of command is the drilling engineer. He is responsible to the superintendent for ensuring that all company rules and regulations, both for operation and maintenance of the drilling rig, are obeyed. He is qualified in all aspects of drilling technology. He is responsible for all training programmes and planning and supervising a drilling programme from the start ("spud-in") to completion. A senior drilling engineer earns about £25,000 a year.

The tool pusher

On the rig the man in charge is the tool pusher. He is in command of everything so long as drilling is taking place. If the rig is to be moved to another location or if drilling stops for bad weather, he then hands over to the barge superintendent, who is usually a master mariner.

The tool pusher will have had long experience in the oil industry in many parts of the world. He will probably be a graduate in mechanical or petroleum engineering. He will have worked his way up through many years as a driller and by attending training courses on drilling technology.

◄ The driller, in the foreground, is controlling drilling operations from his "dog house" while in the background roughnecks are at work on the drill floor.

The tool pusher is directly responsible for all work done by the driller and his crew. He is answerable to the drilling superintendent for the efficient performance of all drilling operations on the rig. He is employed by the rig owner and will earn between £12,000 and £21,000. Sometimes a rig will have only one tool pusher, who will be "on call" 24 hours a day in case of emergencies.

The driller

The man who actually does the drilling is, surprisingly enough, simply called a driller. He operates all the controls from his "dog house" on the drill floor and is responsible for making the hole. This is a highly technical position and often the driller will have an engineering degree, as well as much experience.

It takes about five years for a man to become an efficient driller, for the job involves many different things. For example, he must keep an eye on the quality of the drilling mud. He must know how fast the hole is being drilled, the weight of the bit and when it needs to be changed. And he must always be on the lookout for things that could go wrong with the equipment or the hole. He also keeps the driller's log which records everything that has happened during his shift. He will earn about £15,000 a year.

The roughnecks

Then come the work-force: the semi-skilled men, the roughnecks, derrickmen and crane operators. The roughneck works on the drill floor, handling casing, pipe and the "tongs", a wrench for tightening or loosening the connection between sections of drill pipe.

There are not many pre-entry training courses for roughnecks, although one is being organized in Scotland which will eventually cover many aspects of a drill team. There are courses in the United States, in Holland and in France.

In general, companies prefer to train their own men. One company did open a training school in Scotland when it needed to train 600 men for seven new rigs on a six month course. The qualities they looked for were maturity, good physique and a practical mind. It is often found that ex-servicemen or seamen fall into this category. Roughnecks are really rightly named. There is not much time for sitting around on a drill floor. The roughneck will earn about £8,000 a year, which is some £500 less than the derrickman.

◀ A drilling team in order of seniority. (The numbers refer to the numbers on their helmets.)
1 Drilling superintendent **2** Drilling engineer **3** Tool pusher **4** Driller **5** Roughnecks **6** Roustabouts

The roustabouts

Last in the team comes the man-of-all-work, the general labourer, known as the roustabout. He simply joins either by recommendation (which the companies like) or through a recruiting campaign. This is an unskilled position and the roustabout does all the dirty work, from labouring on the rig floor to chipping paint. His gross pay is around £6,000 a year. This position has a high turnover, as young men who join up thinking it is going to be a glamorous job rapidly become disillusioned.

The mud engineer

Behind this team, but an essential part of it, is the mud engineer. This is a highly specialized position. He is usually a graduate in petroleum engineering and is responsible for the composition and technicalities of the drilling fluid — the mud. He will work very closely with the driller and the geologists.

Pay and conditions

A word of warning should be given about the pay figures quoted above. These are intended only as a very rough guide. So far only a minority of the people working on drilling rigs belong to a trade union and there is no standard rate of pay for the various jobs. The rates vary considerably from company to company, as do the methods of payment. Some companies pay on a weekly, or monthly rate, others on a daily or an hourly rate. A normal working shift is 12 hours, and of this the first eight hours will be at the basic rate, and the rest at time and a half, with all of Saturday at that rate and Sunday at double rate (there are no rest days on an oil rig). Then there are extra allowances.

Another point to bear in mind is that working on an oil rig may not be a life-long career for the lower-paid workers and few companies offer them non-professional pensions. Working on an offshore rig especially is a young man's job. One company estimates that 80 per cent of its crews are under 30 and 50 per cent are under 25 though there is no maximum age limit. The minimum age for starting work, under law, is 18 years.

Beneath the waves

Oil exploration and production from under the sea calls for an increasing number of divers. In 1971, for example, there were 80 divers operating in the North Sea. Now there are 1500, more than half operating at depths of 100 metres and over.

The divers work at varying depths depending on the jobs they have to do. In shallow waters divers simply use wet suits and breathing apparatus and work freely. They live on board the rig or platform, waiting to be called upon for a particular operation.

But in deeper waters, divers cannot just dive down, do the job and return. They are working at pressures very much greater than the pressure at the surface, and they must be returned to atmospheric pressure very slowly to allow their bodies to adjust to the changes. This process is known as decompression.

Below 45 metres saturation diving is used. This is a system under which the diver's body is "saturated" with inert gas, a mixture of oxygen and helium. It gets its name from the fact that after 12 hours the tissues in the human body are saturated and do not absorb any more gas. So after that time, the total decompression period does not change. Time is money in the oil industry and during decompression the divers are not working. Under saturation diving, the six divers live in a decompression chamber on the seabed and simply go to and from the work site in a diving bell. They can stay at depths of 350 metres for two to three weeks, working six hours a day. Decompression only takes place when the job is finished. This must be done slowly. For every 30 metres the diver goes down, he must stay approximately one day in decompression.

Life in a decompression chamber can cause problems. Space is cramped for six men to spend three weeks together. For their part, the men eat, rest and relax, by playing chess, reading or doing jigsaws.

Diving is a dangerous business, unless great care is taken. Since 1971, 40 divers have died in the North Sea alone, mostly through human error or equipment failure. There are psychological and physical problems. If decompression takes place too quickly the diver can suffer from a serious sickness, commonly known as "the bends". Deep sea diving has brought new problems, which include the effect of the cold, diseases of the bone and ear complaints.

Slowly but surely governments have been bringing in stringent safety regulations. All diving must now be under the control of a diving supervisor. Divers must have a UK Health and Safety Executive certificate. Notice must be given to the government for deep dives. All divers must pass strict medical tests. A "flying doctor" service is maintained for the whole of the North Sea.

Aids to underwater work

This diagram gives some indication of the latest developments in underwater operations.

Diving is rapidly moving into the space age. New techniques are being evolved all the time to enable men to spend longer and longer periods in ever-deeper waters.

But even more significant advances are being made in the development of unmanned or remote controlled devices for use in deep waters.

1 The saturation diving system with divers working from a diving bell operated from the platform or supply boat is already in common use.

2 A submarine with manipulator arms shown in action below.

3 In the future unmanned remote controlled vehicles operated from the surface may be able to perform all the operations that a diver could do.

▼ This space-age machine may well be in common use for underwater work in the future. Its manipulator arms, rather like the artificial arms for human beings, can be made to cut steel cables, operate valves or remove obstacles.

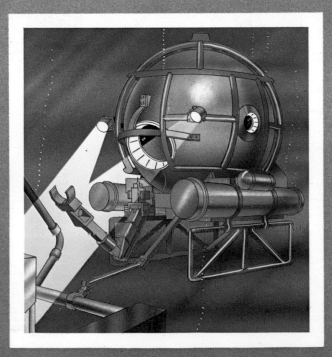

◀ Divers inspecting a pipeline in the tropical waters of the Caribbean Sea. Routine inspections are carried out regularly and divers have to know how to make any necessary repairs.

▼ Divers and attendants look on from the deck of an oil rig support ship as one of their team is gently lowered into the water. He is making a shallow dive so has no need of a diving bell.

▲ Working in the murky depths of the North Sea is far from glamorous. Divers often wear wet suits under their hot water suits to protect them from the cold.

The divers

Deep sea diving equipment

- mask
- back pack
- hot water suit
- chest weight
- safety harness
- lifeline

Oilfield diving has become a highly specialized and highly technical business. A modern diving company will have engineers, technicians, welders, doctors, electronic engineers, diving supervisors and geologists among its staff. The army of people and the sophisticated equipment involved make diving extremely expensive. It costs £8,000 to keep a diver on the sea bottom for one hour's work. A good reliable diver can earn £25,000 a year. But he earns it. Every time the diver goes into the water he knows his life depends directly on his equipment, the surface crew and his fellow divers. Diving is a highly disciplined team effort.

What makes a good diver?

Recruitment for divers today is very selective. It has not always been so. In the early days there was such a demand for divers that partly trained and unskilled men were used. Today efforts are being made to work out the personality of a good diver, and the type of temperament which makes an individual unlikely to panic. Mental fitness is just as important as physical fitness. Experience also counts for a lot. Divers are constantly learning new techniques in the art of diving and ways of avoiding possible dangers. One U.S. diver has a motto on his office wall "The more you know the longer you live". This is so true.

But diving is only half the job. The diver must also be a skilled workman. The diving bell or submersible is simply a vehicle to get him to his place of work and support him. Divers take photographs; they operate electronic devices for testing steelwork or pipes; they place or repair equipment; they fit connectors to pipelines; they weld. For these jobs they must know how to use tools like sledgehammers, wrenches, pipe cutters, welding equipment and cameras. They have to know how a structure is constructed and how complicated production equipment works. They must have some knowledge of mechanics, engineering, the use of explosives and reading a blueprint.

▲ A diver, surrounded by his team of helpers, adjusts his mask before being lowered into the water in a cage.

A diver's routine

On a saturation dive, a diver will wear cotton shorts and a T-shirt while descending. He will take with him enough clothes, books, shaving gear, sweets, or tobacco to chew (no smoking allowed) to last for three weeks.

A saturation diving system is made up of a diving bell, an interlock where the divers leave their suits and flippers, a chamber in which the six divers live and a decompression chamber. Then there is a life support system and a control room.

When a diver moves into the diving bell he will take some food, for he may be working in the water for ten hours. Each diving complex has a service hatch through which food can be sent down and refuse lifted out.

Cold is the enemy of the diver. Some wear wet suits under their hot water suit. (Electrically heated suits have been tried, but proved unsatisfactory — some divers were burned.) Communications with the surface are difficult. A "Donald Duck" effect is produced as the speech sound becomes garbled and an unscrambler is needed to make the words clear.

A good diver will like to have his own equipment. He will have with him patching material for the suit, silicone grease for the zips and talcum powder for suit storage. He will have two extra rings fitted to his weight belt for securing his tools, and a safety harness. He will work methodically, steadily, and not allow himself to be hurried by the "time is money" factor of the oil industry.

The work is infinitely varied. Some days a diver may make one inspection routine dive. At other times he will be working hard, ten hours a day, repairing pipelines, locating and removing debris, inspecting equipment and so on.

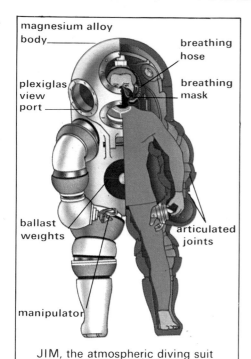

magnesium alloy body

breathing hose

plexiglas view port

breathing mask

ballast weights

articulated joints

manipulator

JIM, the atmospheric diving suit that enables divers to work at depths of up to 500 metres without the need for decompression. It weighs 500 kilos!

New developments

Modern research is aimed at perfecting the one atmosphere diving suit which will allow a diver to work at great depths without the need for decompression afterwards. This means that the diver can go straight down, do the job and surface immediately. Divers wearing the British designed JIM suit have dived to a record 440 metres offshore Spain. As work moves into deeper depths, 600 metres and more, remote controlled submersibles operated from the surface and capable of carrying out the work, are being used. At the same time one-man submersibles, with remote control capability, are being developed.

Training

In 1982 the UK government withdrew its financial support to the Underwater Training Centre at Fort William in Scotland. It believed that the diving industry should finance it. There are two commercial diving schools, but in addition to these, various diving companies operate their own training schools. One French company, for example, has a large training complex at Marseilles which covers every aspect from the training of the raw recruit to advanced diving techniques. It also has training equipment in Aberdeen and Stavanger in Norway.

Timetable for a bounce dive

A bounce dive is one in which divers are taken down to their work place in a diving bell, and brought straight up again afterwards to a decompression chamber at the surface.

▲ 1 Two divers are lowered to the job site inside a bell which is at atmospheric pressure, that is the same pressure as at the surface.

▲ 2 When the bell is in position and the job sighted through the port holes, the diver who is going to do the job puts on his diving gear. Both men are already in diving suits so he simply has to put on fins, back pack and his diving mask.

The second diver, the bellman, is to stay in the bell and tend the diver. He monitors the gas supply and can if necessary leave the bell to go to the help of the diver. The bellman informs the surface that they are ready to "pressure up". High pressure gas brings the pressure inside the bell equal to that outside.

▼ 6 On the rig the bell is "mated" to a decompression chamber which has been brought to the same pressure as the bell. Here the divers carry out the decompression schedule "in comfort".

▲ 5 The bellman informs the surface, the pressure is locked inside and the bell is lifted straight to the surface.

▼ 4 The diver tells the surface he is ready to return to the bell. The supervisor then tells the bellman who helps the diver back in and removes his equipment.

▼ 3 Having been given the go-ahead by the surface supervisor, the diver leaves the bell and begins the job. As he moves away from the bell, the bellman pays out the lifeline, the umbilical. The job is finished in 15 minutes.

Difficult conditions

One of the major problems the oil industry has to face is that generally the regions where oil is found are very inaccessible and suffer from extremely harsh weather conditions. The North Sea is one such region.

In the North Sea gale force winds whip up mountainous seas. In winter months winds of 70–80 knots with waves 20 metres or more in height are frequent. Even in summer winds of 50 knots can spring up. But running casing down a hole can only be done in seas up to 6 metres high. Wind limits for operating a crane are usually 30 to 35 knots. So in bad weather the drilling has to stop. The riser – the flexible connection between the rig and the seabed – is pulled and the drill string "hung off". It is more than helpful to have sufficient warning to be able to carry out this operation. But the North Sea is often very unpredictable.

Bad weather can also affect moving a rig from one location to another. One rig was once known to wait six months for fine weather. A drilling rig can complete a well and then lose 18 days before the anchors can be lifted. It can cost £50,000 a day to hire a drilling rig, with another £12,000 a day expenditure for drilling and supplies. So time is money.

The rigs receive the best possible weather forecasting but meteorology is still an uncertain science. Information is fed into weather forecasting centres from all over Europe and the Atlantic and passed on to the rigs. In return the rigs and platforms send in regular reports as to what is actually happening. What they want to know is what is going to happen . . . and when. Every piece of weather is studied, digested and assessed. Some companies specializing in forecasting put out twice-daily reports to oil companies.

▲ Sometimes the weather in the North Sea is so bad, with high cross winds, that the helicopter cannot land. But so essential is it to maintain the supply line and the relief crews that men are landed or picked up by the winching method. This is a tricky operation and it has been used to lift an injured man, strapped to a stretcher.

▶ All packed up and nowhere to go. In thick fog helicopters are unable to take off for the North Sea rigs, and oilmen may have to spend long and monotonous hours at Aberdeen Heliport waiting for the weather to clear

◄ Surrounded on three sides by jungle and on the other by water, this drilling camp on a tributary of the Amazon in Peru is far from accessible. In such conditions the helicopter is an invaluable lifeline.

But bad weather is not exclusive to the North Sea. In the desert, sandstorms can last a week; in the Arctic snow and blizzards can blow for a week. Hurricanes sweep through the South China Sea, off the Philippines and career across to the Gulf of Mexico. Icebergs are hazards in the Arctic. Off the north-west coast of Australia is "Cyclone Alley". Here in the season, from January to March, there can be up to six cyclones with winds of 120 knots and 21-metre seas.

In all these areas good weather forecasting is important. A constant watch is kept on the path of cyclones and if one comes into the "red zone", a circle 640 km around the rig, drilling is stopped and the rig evacuated. Satellite photographs are taken and studied twice a day; meteorological forecasts are monitored. But even they are limited by the state of the science itself. In less developed areas, operations are hampered by lack of good reporting and forecasting, as well as the uncertainty of the weather itself.

▲ A Hercules aircraft about to take off after unloading supplies at a drilling camp in Alaska. For days at a time the aircraft is the only link with the outside world for the workers at the camp. And bad weather conditions may prevent even the plane from landing.

◄ An island in a sea of sand. This mobile caravan site is "home" for the drillers at a Saudi Arabian drilling camp. Not only do they have to put up with the isolation; sandstorms can strike without warning and last for as long as a week.

Life aboard a platform or rig

One thing in the oil industry is certain. Life on a £60 million offshore drilling rig is far from glamorous or romantic. For 70 men (and the occasional woman geologist) it is home – for roustabouts, roughnecks, tool pushers, drillers, cranemen, engineers, radio operators, divers and cooks. They may well be a "United Nations", an international group of Americans, Britons, Spaniards, Germans and Italians.

But it is also a place of work. It is hard, dirty, physical, heavy work, often in filthy and atrocious weather. The hours are long. It is lonely, living in isolation on that tiny island of steel on the restless sea. It is a monotonous life. At work, asleep, watching a film or television in a comfortable lounge, no one is ever far away from the constant thudding of machinery, throughout the day and night.

Shifts are 12 hours long in 24 hours, night and day. Tours of duty vary from rig to rig. On some it will be seven days on, seven days off. On others it can be 14 days on and 14 days off. Some companies only pay the men while they are actually working on the rig, though meals, accommodation and transport are free. Senior men are usually on contract.

The vital factor, the one that keeps a man working on a rig or platform, is food. If standards of food and accommodation are not up to scratch he will quickly move on to another company. Companies know that contented personnel work better as a team. The men expect plenty of good, high quality food. Second class will not do. "If a man wants two 12 oz. steaks that is what he gets", says a spokesman for one of the big British caterers operating worldwide. But talk of "five star hotel" quality food and accommodation is nonsense. A drilling rig (or a production platform) is not a holiday camp.

Accommodation on a typical production platform, 200 metres high, is on four decks. It consists of small single and double berth cabins; quiet rooms on each deck; a television room and cinema and a mess room for 48, plus small canteens for the 24-hour supply of coffee, tea, coke, ice cream and snacks.

High standards of discipline in cleanliness are insisted upon. Changing rooms are positioned just inside the accommodation area, so that the men do not take their dirty work clothes to their quarters.

No alcohol is allowed on the majority of rigs, for safety reasons. There is a games room with billiards, cards, magazines, darts, television and even in some cases a small "library" of paperbacks. But there really is not much time for recreation. Men are expected to work flat out on their shift . . . They do.

▲ Arriving at the platform by helicopter for another tour of duty. Throughout the tour the helicopter will provide a welcome link with the outside world. Not only does it carry essential supplies, it also brings a regular delivery of letters and newspapers.

▼ Travelling by cage lift is a common means of transport from rig to supply boat. The crane operator must take extra care when he has a human load on board!

▼ Cabins are functional with originally either two or four men sharing. Today regulations insist on only two-men cabins. Tidiness is essential in such a confined space.

▼ Working on an oil rig may give you the opportunity of seeing films you have missed first time round. Films are shown regularly and are usually changed twice a week.

▲ Men unloading casing from a supply vessel on to a production platform. Much of the work on a rig is hard, physical labour involving lifting heavy pieces of equipment. Physical fitness and strength is essential in this kind of work.

▲ A self-service dining room on a production platform. At meal times men can get together in a relaxed, informal atmosphere. And of course they can always be sure of getting plenty of good, well-cooked food — at any time of the day or night.

Fire!

Blow out! That is the cry that oilmen fear. For a blow out can be disastrous. It can start fires which can rage at terrific temperatures for months on end. It can destroy an entire rig. It can cause the loss of great amounts of oil and gas. It can cost a lot of money. It can cause death.

A review of major casualties to oil rigs includes these stark reports:

1972   Transworld Rig 60. Submersible jack-up drilling platform. In South Pass area offshore Louisiana. Blow out followed by fire. Crew evacuated. Platform capsized and sank.

1974   Rig 42. On location off Brunei. Blow out followed by fire. Reported total loss.

1975   Umm Shaif Topper III. Non-propelled jack-up drilling barge. At High Island, Gulf of Mexico. Capsized reportedly due cratering of seabed following blow out of exploratory well.

A blow out happens during drilling when the bit unexpectedly bites into a high pressure gas zone. It usually occurs in areas of unstable rock formation. The drilling mud is too light to withstand the pressure of the gas which forces its way up the casing and blows out. There are gas logging units which can give a warning of blow out and these should be connected to the driller's console in the dog house. There have been great strides in the development of blow-out preventers which can shut off a well in an emergency within seconds. But accidents can happen and ways must be found of dealing with them when they do.

One of the famous names in the oil industry is that of Red Adair of Houston, Texas. He has become a by-word in fighting blow outs and controlling wild wells. His company's motto is "Around the clock around the world". That just about sums it up. For a call may come to his office at any hour of the day or night. It may come from Texas or California or from Iraq or Nigeria or the middle of the Sahara desert. His company deals with about 30 fires and blow outs a year.

He gathers together his team of key men and they are on the next aircraft. Every job is different. Sometimes in remote places the team, flown in with their specialized equipment, have to train a fire crew from local workers who are probably terrified by the intensity of the fire.

In 1965 saboteurs in the Sahara blew up five wells. Red was called in and his team set up their tents in the desert. Sandstorms delayed the work; food had to be flown in. Four weeks, and a million lost barrels of oil later, they put out the last of the five fires.

On another occasion 16 wells on one platform all caught fire in the Gulf of Mexico. A series of floating platforms were built by a construction and engineering firm in Houston, Texas. These platforms were then nudged towards the blazing platform so that the Adair team could gradually approach it. During the operation the platform was deluged with water from 100 metres away.

▼ In May, 1951 fire broke out at this well-head at Naft Safid, Iran. It lasted for 43 days before it was finally put out.

Blowing out a well-head fire
One of the methods of dealing with a fire is simply to blow it out. A plan of action has been drawn up and men and machines have gathered at the scene of this desert well-head fire. First an explosive charge is prepared. An empty oil drum is packed with explosive wrapped in asbestos sheeting.

◄ A spectacular fire on a production platform in the Persian Gulf off the coast of Dubai, November 1973. The fire raged for weeks before being brought under control.

▼ BP's fire-fighting ships patrol around the production platforms in the North Sea. This ship was converted from a tanker at a cost of £5 million.

▲ With its detonator leads trailing from it, the drum is gently nosed out on the end of a boom. All the while hoses are spraying water on to the whole well-head area to reduce the heat. If there is no water available, then a well must first be drilled.

▲ When the drum is about 3 metres above the roaring well-head, the charge is detonated. If all goes well the fire is literally blown out. But the most dangerous part is yet to come, for the well must be capped and gas may still be gushing from it.

▲ After a lot more cooling of the area by water, the team has to clear away all the chewed-up well-head equipment. The well is then capped off by attaching a new valve assembly and making it fast. The fire has been safely brought under control.

Safety: the vital factor

An offshore drilling rig is a factory. Its product is a "hole". It is equipped with heavy machinery, cranes, electricity, drilling equipment, compressors, pumps. It is exposed to gales, to waves, to snow, ice and fog. On board some 80 workers toil . . . and live.

As in any land-based factory there are accidents. Cranes break; cranes fall into the sea; men get hurt; fires break out; men get killed. But unlike a factory a rig can also be torn from its anchorage in a gale. It can find itself drifting, without power, about the ocean while tugs strive to get a towline on board. Rigs can sink. In the last 20 years there have been more than 70 major rig disasters throughout the world. More than 100 men lost their lives. Thirty rigs have been lost.

Rigs do have lifeboats and survival capsules. But it is essential that crews are fully trained in their use. The United States Coastguard has now taken steps to ensure practical training and testing. Two helicopters and a ship can make spot checks on rigs. This followed the sinking in 1976 of a rig under tow in a violent storm. One survival capsule was attached to a tug by two lines from the top of the capsule. The tug and capsule continually banged against each other. So one of the men in the capsule threw off one line. Shortly after he had re-entered the capsule, it capsized, drowning 13 men.

The campaign for safety is being stepped up however. Inspectors of the UK Department of Energy visit rigs to check on all aspects of safety, including cranes, and fire-fighting and life-saving equipment. But the inspectors are few in number. They have no way of making a surprise visit, as they have to give advance warning to obtain a place in a company helicopter.

By law, a stand-by safety boat has to be on-station for every drilling rig and production platform in the North Sea. Day and night, 24 hours a day, seven days a week, it simply circles round and round in case of emergencies. Usually these stand-by boats are manned by ex-fishermen.

Training courses to deal with the problem of safety have been introduced. The Offshore Survival Unit of the Robert Gordon's Institute of Technology at Aberdeen, for example, runs regular five-day survival courses. These cover personal survival techniques, the use of emergency radio and signals and the handling of lifeboats.

The Petroleum Industry Training Board runs a four-day fire-fighting course in Scotland. Nineteen companies have sent men for training, including men from Spain, France, Ireland, Norway, Venezuela, Mauritius, Australia and New Zealand. A special fire-training college is to be built, financed by a number of oil companies.

▲ This self-propelled survival capsule is unsinkable and can negotiate flame-covered waters without damage. It holds up to 14 men.

▼ In 1976 the semi-submersible rig "Deep Sea Driller" ran aground off Norway while being towed from site for repairs. Conditions at the time were 80 knot winds, heavy seas and a blizzard. Of the 50 men on board, six were killed and 17 injured.

In March 1976 a drillship was removing the blow-out preventer stack from a completed well in the Gulf of Mexico. The stack was being hoisted on deck when it suddenly fell back into the sea through the moon pool, carrying with it four men who had climbed onto it to secure steadying lines. Only one of the men made it back to the ship.

◄ Workmen on the drillship "Pelican" off Labrador fastening the cables attached to the blow-out preventer. The men are all wearing safety harnesses, a very necessary precaution when working above the "moon pool" with the waters swirling below.

▼ A blow-out preventer stack of the type used on land rigs. This series of valves can close around the drill string or across the entire hole if high pressure gas rushes up from below. On offshore rigs the B.O.P. stack is usually placed on the seabed.

Supplies and services

Helicopter pilot

The lifeline between a drilling rig, whether it be in the North Sea or in the Indonesian jungle, is the helicopter. The helicopter is the daily "express train" service to the rig, ferrying relief crews and vital supplies in two hours, a journey which may take the "goods train"—the supply boat—two days. It is the "flying ambulance" if an injured man needs to be ferried to hospital. In the jungle it is the "removal van" for the whole drilling rig, which is taken to pieces and air-lifted to its new location, in what may be as many as 400 loads.

Without helicopters the oil industry today could not operate. In 1981, more than 650,000 passengers were carried by helicopter from Scotland to North Sea rigs and platforms. In all, some 150 machines are operating in this region. A pilot's earnings are between £10,000 and £15,000 a year. Some companies will have a helicopter on call, 24 hours a day, at a cost of £500,000 a year, simply to meet an emergency call for a vital spare part for machinery to keep the drilling going.

Landing on the tiny helideck of a rig, between derricks and aerials, is a tricky business. High winds, snow and ice are all common hazards and fog frequently causes delays. The hours the pilots can legally work are limited to a maximum of 50 in a seven-day period or 160 hours in 28 days. But these are subject to alteration.

Besides the drillers, the roughnecks, the divers, there is an army of other people at work behind the scenes, whose jobs are vital to the smooth running of an oil rig. Helicopter pilots and supply boat crew bring the food and equipment without which no rig can operate. Crane operators perform difficult and often dangerous manoeuvres to get equipment and supplies from the boat to the rig and to move drilling gear around the rig floor. Cooks make an important contribution to the health and well-being of the crew. And medical staff are on hand in case of an emergency. Without the support of all these people, 24 hours a day, work on the rig would grind to a halt.

▼ A helicopter pilot preparing to land on the helideck.

Supply boat crew

The "plodders" are the supply boats, tough, rugged vessels, especially designed to battle their way through mountainous seas and gale force winds, carrying the essential heavy supplies: chemicals for the mud, pipe casing and so on. Work on board is a dangerous business. Unloading in rough weather can be very risky and in some cases supply boats have crashed into the rig structures, causing damage to the legs and to the cranes.

A typical 90-day exploration well is likely to require the movement of 3,000 tonnes of material ranging from fresh water, fuel and drill pipe to foodstuffs and clothing.

Around the world there are some 150 companies in the supply boat and tug boat operations. They have about 2,400 vessels, valued at about £1,600 million.

Crews vary in the North Sea operations; some companies employ a large number of Spaniards under British skippers. Most of the captains have had deep sea experience but, as one put it, "nothing I had ever done before prepared me for the actual physical hard work necessary on a supply boat to handle her in all weathers".

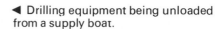

Crane operators

The crane operator is an important link in the chain of operations. Most operators had no experience of lifting objects from the deck of a bouncing supply ship hundreds of metres below them. Timing has to be absolutely accurate. There have been cases where cranes have toppled into the sea.

The crane operator has an important role in the drilling crew. In all weathers he moves pieces about the rig to the drill floor, such as pipe from the storage deck. Most rigs will have two cranes, one 25-tonne revolving crane and one 34-tonne. Five-day basic training courses for crane operators are now run by the Scottish Offshore Training Association.

The medics

Career opportunities for medical staff are limited in the oil industry. No full-time doctors are employed on drilling rigs. But a company doctor will usually visit a rig once a month to check up on hygiene and cleanliness. According to British law all rigs must have at least one medically trained person (two if there are more than 40 people on board). He must be either a registered nurse, or an enrolled nurse, or the holder of a certificate of competence who has received adequate training in the mechanical artificial respiration equipment which must be carried on board. The Scottish Offshore Training Association runs courses for obtaining the certificate and refresher courses.

Safety, health and welfare regulations require that there should be a "sick bay" and list the medical stores and medicines which must be kept. In an emergency the first-aid man can take instructions from a shore-based doctor while a helicopter pick-up is being arranged. It has been suggested that all rigs should have a State Registered Nurse on board. But the chief medical officer of a world-wide company commented, "If you put an SRN on a rig he would be sitting there with a thermometer in one hand and an enema in the other waiting for a case. People on rigs are normally fit. They have pre-employment and two-yearly check-ups. An ex-service sick bay attendant is the ideal sort of person. He is used to doing other jobs when he's not needed. He's not going to sit around and wait for a casualty because the chances are there won't be one".

Cooks

Catering on an oil rig is a highly specialized business. It is usually sub-contracted at a fixed price for a specified number of people. The sub-contractors provide food and staff and offer advice on equipment and layout of kitchens and cabins.

It needs a high level of organization to supply men with 12 meals, during a full 24-hour day, seven days a week, on a two-shift basis. Usually a five weeks' supply of canned and frozen food in sub-zero storage is kept to meet emergencies. That is in case the helicopters and supply boats cannot get through to the rig because of bad weather. But the emphasis is on fresh food, prepared on board. All rigs have a baker who provides fresh rolls, bread, cakes and pastries. The daily helicopter brings the light and perishable goods. General provisions and equipment come in the supply boat.

People working on the catering side enter the trade through the usual channels; the cooks will have received the same training as cooks in any hotel or restaurant. This involves courses at technical or catering colleges, followed by experience in various positions in hotels, restaurants and so on.

▼ The cook has to cater for healthy appetites!

Islands in the sea

The drilling rig has completed the holes. The oil company has decided that it will be a money-making venture to develop the field. The next step is to make a production plan. This is a detailed and complicated operation. It calls for a production platform. This will drill more wells, production wells, to drain the field economically and efficiently. At the same time the platform controls the flow of oil from the field. Platforms vary considerably in size and complexity according to the depth of water, the size of the field and weather conditions. Some fields may need only one platform, others require many more.

Production platforms are, in fact, islands in the sea. They house all the equipment needed to get the oil out and pump it ashore. They have facilities to remove water from the oil, and to flare the gas that cannot be piped ashore. They are the place of work and "home" for the 100 or more men who live and work there. These include the drilling teams, mud engineers, geologists, electricians, mechanics, welders, divers, pumpmen and, of course, cooks.

Life on a platform is much the same as on a drilling rig, except that there are more jobs to do. It is a case of living on the job all the time. In some fields now, separate "hotel" platforms are being built, for safety reasons, as some governments argue that it is unsafe to have men living on a platform that is producing oil.

Platforms can be made of steel or concrete and are massive structures. Steel platforms can be up to 150 metres high and weigh more than 50,000 tonnes. Concrete platforms are even heavier. It can take 345,000 tonnes of concrete and 23,000 tonnes of steel to build them. They are built in the upright position on shore, then floated out and finished in deep water before being towed to the field by as many as six tugs. Sometimes the modules for the living quarters are put in place before tow-out. These platforms are held in place by their great weight and are thus known as "concrete gravity platforms". Some have storage facilities for oil in their base. Concrete platforms are used in deeper water. They have to be built to stay in place for as long as 25 years, the average life of a field.

Once the platform is in position, the production wells are drilled by directional drilling. The final act is to set in place the well-head and the "Christmas tree". This is a series of valves which control the well pressure and the flow of oil.

As oil is discovered in deeper waters, plans are being developed to place on the seabed all the equipment needed to produce the oil. The equipment will be remotely controlled, and may do away altogether with a platform.

Production platforms and sea depths (depth in metres)

flare stack

North Sea platform

work boat

300

250

200

80

150

100

50

seabed

well risers

piles

◀ Building production platforms for the North Sea involved new techniques that had not been needed in shallower waters.

▼ Constructing a steel platform
The jacket of a steel platform, basically the legs, is constructed on shore on its side. It is then towed to the field on flotation tanks by tugs.

▼ By carefully controlled flooding of the flotation tanks, the jacket is up-ended until its legs are resting on the seabed.

▼ The legs are pinned to the bed by steel piles. Then the modules, the houses for equipment and men, are lifted on by huge floating cranes.

Directional drilling

It can require as many as 50 production wells to develop even a moderately sized oilfield. Building a production platform for each well would be far too costly, so techniques have been evolved by which a large number of wells can be drilled from a single platform. This calls for directional drilling. The first 100 or so metres are drilled vertically until the "kick-off" point is reached. Then the hole is "bent" from the vertical at an angle of up to 50°. Wells which are only 35 metres apart at the platform can be 8 km apart by the time they reach oil-bearing rock 2.5 km down.

The diagram on the right shows how a typical oilfield is tapped. Four production platforms each with roughly 20 wells drilled from them in all directions ensure that the field is exploited to the full. The drill deck of each platform has a number of slots in it and the derrick is "skidded" from one slot to the next to drill the holes required. The oil is piped to one central platform and from there piped to shore.

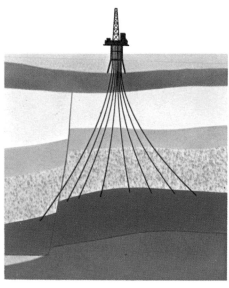

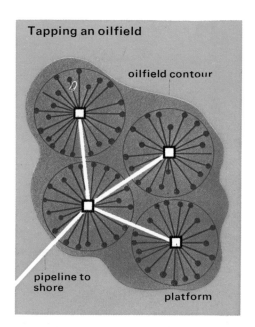

Tapping an oilfield

oilfield contour

pipeline to shore

platform

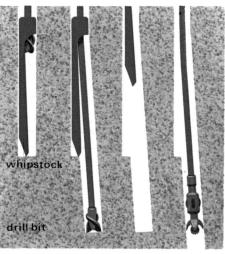

whipstock

drill bit

▲ When the "kick-off" point is reached, the correct angle for drilling is worked out by means of a magnetic compass and a camera. Then a whipstock, a simple steel wedge, is set in at the bottom of the hole, "forcing" the bit to drill off in the required direction.

▼ In the early days of exploration at sea, drilling was confined to the shallow seas of the Mediterranean, the Persian Gulf and the Gulf of Mexico. Today, thanks to technology introduced by North Sea drillers, oil companies all over the world are moving into deeper water.

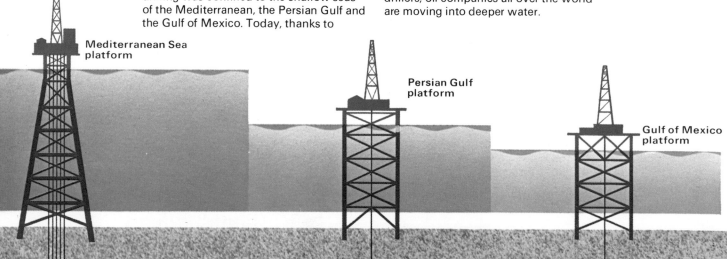

Mediterranean Sea platform

Persian Gulf platform

Gulf of Mexico platform

The pipeline

The usual atlas maps of Europe, of America, of Russia, Asia, China, Australia, the Middle East, in fact the maps of any country, do not show them . . . the thin lines which criss-cross the countries of the world. These lines are vital to the flow of crude oil from the fields to the terminals, to refineries or tankers. They are vital to the flow of oil products from the refineries to the markets. These are the pipelines of the world.

There are about 1.5 million km of pipelines, 70 per cent carrying natural gas, 20 per cent crude oil and 10 per cent oil products. Like gigantic snakes they cross plains, climb icy mountains, burrow under rivers, writhe across deserts. Sometimes, in remote areas, they can be seen. But most lie buried. The land is restored, crops grow again and grass is sown.

In Holland, when an offshore line came ashore, the whole of the top soil and the plant life was placed in a special nursery and when the line was laid, it was replaced in its original position. For it was an essential part of the sea defences, holding the sand dunes together against the sea. In another part of Holland, special insulation had to be placed around the line, as it ran through some bulb fields. It was thought that heat from the line would disturb the delicate growth pattern of the bulbs.

Pipelines vary from 25 cm to 120 cm in diameter. They may run for a short distance or they may run for more than 1,000 km. Once the line of the route has been agreed (and this may take years), an army of machines moves into action. There are ditch diggers, hoe dippers with "fangs" like some prehistoric monster, hydraulic excavators, trenchers and rock cutters.

The sections of the pipe have to be welded together and then coated with a protective against rust. One machine, a panoramic land crawler, is designed to test the welds during construction. Self-propelled by three motors, it "crawls" along the pipe, stops, idles or reverses as directed by a remote control device. It travels at 14 metres a minute and can work for 10 hours without refuelling.

Because they have different qualities, a number of different oil products can be sent down the same pipeline. They are separated by a "batching pig", a large plastic "ball" which is inserted at source between two different products. The pig flows along at the same rate as the oil and at selected points of the line sets off signalling devices. On arrival at its destination the pig triggers off automatic valve changes and marshals the fluids into batches. Pigs are also used for cleaning the insides of pipelines, to keep them free from rust and waxy deposits.

▼ Construction work on a section of the 480 km pipeline stretching from Trieste, Italy across the Austrian Alps to Ingolstadt, southern Germany. Safety precautions have been taken to prevent soil dislodged during trenching operations from falling onto the road below.

▲ **Beaumaris, Anglesey. May 1974** Work is in progress on the pipeline which will cross the Menai Straits to reach the Welsh mainland, which can be seen in the background.

▼ **Beaumaris, Anglesey. July 1975** This section of the pipeline is complete and there is no trace of the excavations. The land is restored and grass has grown.

▲ In many parts of the world vast areas of jungle or scrub have to be cleared before a pipeline can be laid. The pipeline shown in the process of construction here runs for 1,700 km from Dar Es Salaam in Tanzania to N'dola in Zambia, Africa.

◄ A welder at work on a pipeline in Abu Dhabi. With the sun blazing down on the desert sand it must be hot work.

Piping oil across Alaska

It was in 1968 that oil was first discovered on the North Slope of Alaska, 300 km inside the frozen wastes of the Arctic Circle. Then the problem was how to get it out, to help meet the needs of the oil-hungry Americans. After many environmental and political battles, it was decided to build a pipeline stretching the 1300 km from Prudhoe Bay in the north to the ice-free port of Valdez in the Gulf of Alaska. From there the oil would be shipped in a fleet of 32 tankers, loading at the rate of two a day.

It was an enormous undertaking. At peak periods 18,000 people worked on the pipeline and pumping stations. These included 1,900 women who did every type of work; as labourers, traffic controllers, cooks, surveyors, communications operators, security guards and even welders. Surveyors who mapped the route for the line were dropped by helicopter, and then walked every step of the way, in the appalling Arctic conditions. More than 17,000 machines, valued at £300 million, were used, as well as 14,500 pieces of heavy equipment, worth £285 million. The vast army of machinery, cranes, drills, manipulators and tractors was carried in pieces by cargo-carrying aircraft or by ships from Seattle which could only get through the ice-bound seas for six weeks a year.

More than 650 km of the line is built above ground on supports. Putting up the supports meant drilling 78,000 holes, each 15 metres deep. This elevated pipe is insulated with pre-fabricated jackets of glass fibre bonded to sheet metal. Each panel, 7 metres long, is picked up and folded to shape and then placed round the pipe by a special machine.

The rest of the line is buried. This pipe has a protective coating, too, of specially made tape, and the pipe had to be heated to 90°C before it was wrapped round. The ditch was dug by a gigantic chain saw with a blade 4 metres long.

Alaska is an area of rapid changes of temperature and even earthquakes. These could cause the pipeline to expand and contract to a dangerous degree. So sections of the line are laid in a zig-zag pattern to convert any movement caused by expansion and contraction into a sideways movement. The pipeline design will allow the line to move 6 metres horizontally and 90 cm vertically without rupturing.

Food and living conditions in the construction camps were good. But the work itself was frustrating. According to one worker, "It was like working on an automobile production line. We only saw our little segment, screwing nut 36 on bolt 34. Sometimes a single day was like a month".

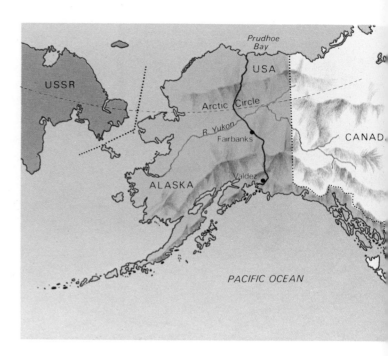

▲ The 1300 km pipeline from Prudhoe Bay to Valdez follows no easy route. It passes through several rugged mountain ranges and crosses several rivers.

▼ The Valdez pipeline terminal in the course of construction. Eventually the terminal will receive 2 million barrels of oil a day. The oil will travel at 11 kph along the pipe and take 4½ days to complete its journey.

▲ More than half of the pipeline is built above the ground on supports, which are frozen in. This is to prevent the oil's heat from thawing the permafrost, which could cause erosion and seriously disturb the growth of vegetation. The elevated pipeline also allows animals such as caribou to pass underneath it.

▼ Welding in the confined space of the pipeline is back-breaking work.

▶ This worker in a pipe storage yard near Fairbanks is well-wrapped up, with even his face covered against the biting cold. Temperatures along the pipeline route range from −60°C in winter to 32°C in the short summer!

▼ A section of the pipe supported by a sideboom (seen in the foreground on the left). The man and the girl on the right are holding propane burners which they use to heat up the pipe to 90°C before its protective tape is wrapped round.

Cold and isolation were not the only problems on the pipeline. On one day 13 bears invaded Pump Station 4, finding their way into the pump houses, the mess room and even the 12 cm pipe! They have become such a pest that Bear Patrols have been set up in some areas.

Bringing the oil ashore

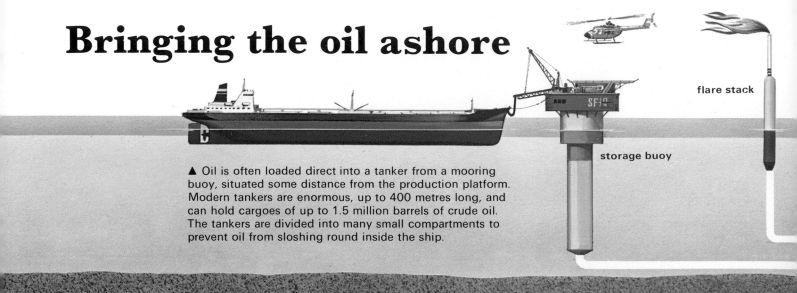

flare stack

storage buoy

▲ Oil is often loaded direct into a tanker from a mooring buoy, situated some distance from the production platform. Modern tankers are enormous, up to 400 metres long, and can hold cargoes of up to 1.5 million barrels of crude oil. The tankers are divided into many small compartments to prevent oil from sloshing round inside the ship.

The oil company has discovered the oil. After much heart-searching and counting the millions of pounds involved, it has decided that it is worthwhile to develop the field. One major hurdle remains – how to get the oil ashore? There are three main methods. The oil can be loaded direct into tankers from a mooring buoy situated about 1.5 km from the platform. It can be stored, either in the platform or separately, and loaded ashore. Or it can be piped all the way beneath the seabed in pipelines.

Underwater pipelines are expensive. It costs well over half a million pounds to lay one single kilometre. But once pipelines are in place there are no continuing costs. First of all the route has to be surveyed and inspected by submarines and divers to make sure there are no major rocks in the way.

Then the lengths of 13-metre pipe are delivered to the pipelaying barge. Before delivery they have been coated with concrete and other materials to protect them and weigh them down. On the barge the lengths of pipe are welded together. The team of welders work in 12-hour shifts for five weeks, and then have one week off. After the welds have been coated to match the previous coating, the pipe is lowered carefully into the water.

Pipelaying requires a small fleet of vessels, including lay barges, trenching barges, survey vessels, diving support craft, supply boats and helicopters. Like all operations it is dependent on weather. In one year from May to December, the total number of working days for three lay barges was 268 days 14 hours, while waiting on weather occupied 216 days 6 hours – a 40 per cent downtime.

Once the pipe has been laid, along come the trenching barges. For the pipe must be buried beneath the seabed, both for its own protection from ships' anchors and trawls, and for the protection of fishing gear.

The line is then given a hydrostatic test in which it is filled with water to a very high pressure and left for 24 hours. Any lessening of the pressure indicates a leak. Further tests are carried out by sending a "pig" through the line. This is not the friendly bacon porker, but a large, round device to test the line. One type, the "Kaliper pig", is almost 2 metres in length and weighs 250 kilos. It is designed to locate, measure and record changes in the inside diameter of the pipe. Two pigs are often used, put in 11 km apart, the second to check up on the first. They travel at about 3 kph and are propelled along by water being pumped in behind them.

▲ A lay barge carefully lowering the pipeline into the water. It will lay about 2 km of pipe a day. Each day during the operation a diver goes down to inspect the pipe.

pressurized welding chamber

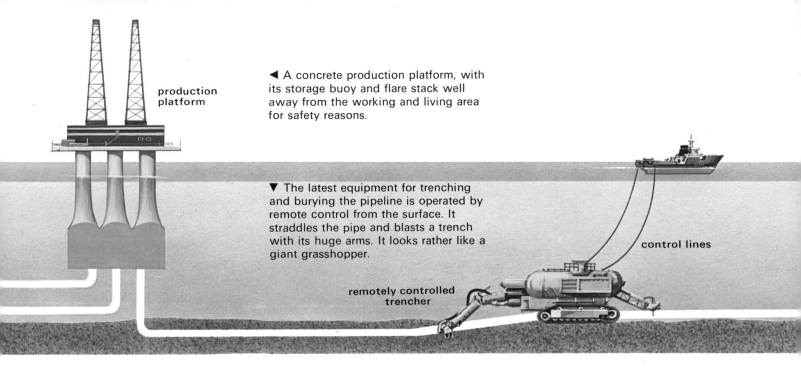

production platform

◄ A concrete production platform, with its storage buoy and flare stack well away from the working and living area for safety reasons.

▼ The latest equipment for trenching and burying the pipeline is operated by remote control from the surface. It straddles the pipe and blasts a trench with its huge arms. It looks rather like a giant grasshopper.

control lines

remotely controlled trencher

◄ This one million barrel concrete storage tank was built in Norway for the Ekofisk field in the North Sea and is the largest of its kind in the world.

▼ A pipe-laying barge showing clearly the ramp, which hangs over the stern and supports the pipe as it enters the water. If the pipe was not supported in this way, it could bend and buckle.

▲ The final link-up of the 176 km underwater pipeline from the Forties field in the North Sea was achieved by a new method, perfected by BP and the Italian company, Saipem. This involved raising the two ends of the pipe and welding in a short length alongside the barge, instead of on the seabed.

◄ If the pipeline has to be repaired divers are sent down. New techniques have been developed by which the divers remove the concrete coating from the pipeline and work on the repair in a pressurized welding chamber. They are professional welders and pipe-fitters who have been specially trained to work in this environment. They wear the same masks and suits as they would for working at the surface.

In future whole sections of new pipeline may be welded together underwater by this method, instead of being welded at the surface and laid underwater in one piece as at present.

to the refinery

The oil refinery

gas

110°C

raw petrols

kerosine and jet fuels

gas oil and diesel oil

bubblecap

heavy gas oil

340°C

furnace

400°C

crude oil

steam

residue

Primary distillation

The crude oil is first heated in a furnace to 400°C. This turns 75 per cent of the oil into gas; the rest remains liquid. The mixture then passes in to the fractionating tower, which is divided up into a series of trays, each containing about 6 cm of liquid. The bubblecaps force the oil vapours rising up the tower to bubble through the liquid. Each of the trays is kept at a lower temperature than the one below it by a flow of cooler liquid from the tray above. When a particle of vapour reaches a tray which is at its boiling point, it condenses and joins the liquid on the tray, to be drawn off for further processing. The heavier oils have a higher boiling point than the lighter oils.

They stand, like science fiction cities, these oil refineries, with weird-shaped, silver-painted columns reaching up into the sky; hundreds of kilometres of pipe snaking over the ground; rows of grey storage tanks; and overall an air of awesome silence, with very few people to be seen. What goes on there?

A typical refinery will, every 24 hours, pump more than 30 million litres of crude oil into the processing units. That crude oil, produced from wells thousands of kilometres away, in the desert, or swamp, or offshore, has to be processed to serve the many needs of man. Like the drillers, refiners have their own language. They speak of "cat crackers", "distillation units" and "fractionating columns".

These are all stages in the process of making the various oil products such as petrol, aviation jet fuels, kerosine, diesel oil, fuel oil, and the liquefied petroleum gases used to make everything from fibres and anti-freeze to paint and plastics.

The operations of a refinery are complex. But basically the equipment is divided into two types: the first separates the products by physical means; the second converts one substance into another by a chemical change.

Primary distillation belongs to the first type. Because crude oil is made up of many different compounds, each boiling at different temperatures, the oil products can be separated by heat.

But primary distillation does not provide enough of the lighter oils such as petrol to satisfy demand. It does, however, produce more of certain heavy oils than are needed. So some of these heavy oils are broken up to make lighter oils in a second process, cat-cracking. This process uses a catalyst, a substance that speeds up a chemical reaction but itself remains unchanged at the end. The oil is mixed with a finely powdered catalyst and heated to a very high temperature. The cracked gases are then separated and collected.

The world oil refining capacity in 1981 was 4,085 million tonnes a year. This exceeds consumption (2,902 million tonnes) as a consequence of world recession, energy saving and use of alternative energy sources.

From the refinery the products are distributed to the different consumers. This calls for careful planning to make sure that the required type and quantity of product is available at the right place at the right time. The products are routed through strategically placed terminals and depots. These are supplied by road tankers, by rail tankers, by ocean-going and coastal tankers, and by underground pipelines.

▲ The panel room of a refinery control centre. The entire operations of the refinery are controlled from this centre, with the aid of a computer and automatic control instruments. The men working there must watch the dials at all times to make sure everything is going smoothly.

▼ A view of a refinery in Finland.

	United States of America	Arabian heavy	Iranian heavy	Arabian light	North Sea	
petrol and chemical feedstock	31%	18%	21%	21%	23%	
kerosine and jet fuels		11.5%	13%	15%	15%	
	16%	18%				
gas oil and diesel oil	14%		20%	21%	24%	
heavy fuel oil	39%	52.5%	46%	43%	38%	

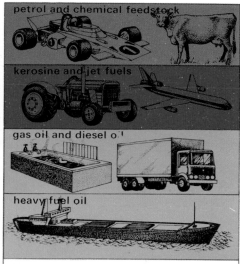

The breakdown of crude oil
Crude oils found in different parts of the world contain different proportions of each constituent.

Reference section

Useful words

Some useful words to know if you are thinking of working on an oil rig.

Anti-clinal traps formed as a result of a fold in which the rock strata become shaped like a house roof. Any oil collects in the angle.

Appraisal well a hole drilled to learn more about the extent and properties of an oil reservoir.

Associated gas gas combined with oil in production. It is removed by gas separators and may be used as fuel for machinery at the well site.

Barge originally a flat-bottomed boat. Now many types for different purposes: drilling, pipelaying, derrick.

Barrel a unit of measurement for oil. In the 19th century oil was shipped in barrels. Today it is transported in bulk by tankers, but the term barrel is still used. One barrel equals 160 litres, or 42 US gallons or 35 Imperial gallons.

B/d barrels per day. The average daily output from a producing well. Multiplied by fifty gives tonnes per year.

B/t barrels per tonne. The specific gravity of oil varies. So does the number of barrels in a tonne. One type may yield 6.6 b/t while heavy oil will yield 5.8. An average is 7.5.

Bends decompression sickness in divers.

Bit actual cutting tool at the end of the drill string. The length of time a bit lasts varies between 25 and 100 hours' drilling.

Black oil a very heavy oil (fuel oil) or dark crude oil.

Block an area licensed to a company or companies for exploration.

A U.K. block is roughly 200–250 sq km.

Blow out accidental escape of oil or gas from a well during the drilling stage.

B.O.P. blow-out preventer. A collection of safety valves, worked by hydraulic action, which automatically closes a well if it is in danger of blowing out.

Bury barge barge used in burying underwater pipe.

Cap rock a layer, e.g. clay or salt which overlies a reservoir rock and prevents leakage of oil to the surface.

Casing steel lining inside the hole to prevent sides caving in.

Casing perforation the holes made in the casing to complete an oil well so that the oil can flow.

Christmas tree collection of pipes and valves at the well head to control the flow of oil.

Clean oil light refined oil products, e.g. motor spirit.

▲ Roughnecks removing a worn drill bit from the drill string at a well on the North Slope, Alaska.

Collar a section of heavy pipe fitted above the drilling bit to give it extra weight.

Concession right to drill for oil on a block obtained under licence from the State.

Cowboy anyone reckless or inexperienced, especially among divers.

Decompression the process by which a diver, after working at depth, under great pressure, breathing helium and oxygen, is returned to normal pressure. This is done in a decompression chamber on the support boat.

Derrick barge barge fitted with large cranes for lifting up to 2,000 tonnes for placing equipment on production platform.

Derrickman member of drilling team who works high up on the derrick handling pipe.

Deviation well well drilled at an angle of up to 50° from the vertical from production platform.

Directional drilling technique used in offshore drilling by which several deviation wells are drilled from one single platform.

Dog house the driller's position and control console on the drill floor.

Downtime time spent waiting for suitable weather to continue work.

Drill string lengths of pipe connecting the bit to the drilling derrick.

Dry hole a hole with little or no trace of oil.

Dynamic positioning method of keeping a drillship over a hole using signals from the seabed and a computer to give orders to propellers and side thrusters.

Fishing operation to recover equipment lost down the hole.

Flaring a process by which associated gas that cannot be re-injected or piped ashore is burned off from the platform.

Fossil fuels fuels such as coal and oil which are produced in the earth over millions of years by the fossilization of plants and animals.

Hyperbaric chamber a compartment which can be sealed and pressurized to reproduce the pressures met by divers. Used for training and decompression.

Jacket legs of a steel platform.

Jack-up drilling rig used in shallow waters with legs which are jacked down to the seabed when drilling.

▲ A jack-up rig being towed out to its first job. Once in position its platform will be jacked up above the level of the water.

Kelly the shaft which engages at one end with the rotary table on the drill floor and at the other with the drill pipe.

Lay barge barge used for laying underwater pipelines.

Migration gradual movement of oil from source rock to a reservoir.

Modules "houses" on a platform containing equipment and accommodation.

Monkey board the platform high up in the derrick from which the derrickman works.

Moon pool the hole on the drill floor through which the drill pipe passes.

Mouse hole a hole drilled under the derrick floor in which a length of drill pipe is temporarily suspended before being connected to the drill string.

Mud a special mixture of chemicals and mud which is pumped through the hollow drill pipe. It controls pressure and returns to the surface with cuttings for examination by geologists.

One atmosphere chamber a pressure chamber used in underwater operations where men, receiving breathing air, live and work in a normal dry atmosphere. Used in deep subsea production systems to allow men to go in and service equipment.

Petrochemicals chemicals produced from crude oil or natural gas.

Pig round metal or plastic instrument used to clean or inspect inside of pipeline. So called because it makes a squealing sound as the blades scrape the side.

Platform large structure of either steel or concrete, containing all equipment for drilling production wells and producing and processing crude oil.

Plugging after drilling, an exploration hole will be plugged with concrete either temporarily or, if dry, permanently.

Primary recovery the production of oil under its natural pressure in the reservoir.

Recoverable resources the amount of oil which can be recovered by present methods. Normally some 40 per cent of oil in a reservoir is recoverable by primary recovery.

Rig structure housing the drilling equipment for exploration drilling.

Riser the pipe which connects the drill floor to the subsea well head, situated on the seabed. It also protects the drill string.

Roughneck member of drill crew, working on drill floor.

Roustabout labourer on drilling rig or platform.

Secondary recovery method by which water is injected or associated gas reinjected into the reservoir of oil, to maintain pressure and enable more oil to be recovered than can be by primary recovery.

Seismic survey method of bouncing back sound waves for obtaining information on depths of rock beneath the surface.

Semi-submersible rig a rig supported on large pontoons submerged in the sea to keep it stable. The semi-submersible is used in deep sea drilling.

Separators machinery on the production platform which separates the water and gas from the oil before it is transported ashore.

Single point buoy mooring system mooring and loading system enabling tankers to load at sea, either direct from a subsea system or via a platform. Usually placed about 1.5 km from the platform.

Source rocks the rocks in which oil was formed before migration.

Spudding in beginning the drilling operation by "making a hole".

Strike first signs of oil in a hole.

Subsea well head used to produce oil from a field instead of from a production platform. As much of the equipment as possible is connected to a central collecting area from the seabed. Developments taking place for use in very deep waters.

Tool pusher man in charge of all drilling operations on a rig.

Well logging record of all data collected while drilling is in progress. Of great use to driller and geologist.

Wild cat speculative exploration well drilled in search of new oil after geological and geophysical surveys.

Wild well a well that is out of control because of a blow out.

General careers information

You now have some idea of the wide range of careers in the oil industry from tool pushers to roughnecks, cooks to welders, mechanical engineers to geologists. If you are thinking of a career how can you set about it? And what does the recruitment officer of an oil company or a drilling contractor look for?

There is no easy entry into the oil business. It is possible to begin at the bottom as a roustabout, which is just about the only unskilled job there is. To do this you should approach drilling contractors direct rather than oil companies. In general it is the drilling contractors who own the rigs and lease them out to oil companies, for exploration, complete with crew.

You can, by hard work, experience and keeping your wits about you, be promoted to a roughneck or a derrickman. You will attend courses run by the company. For example, a Drilling Technology Training Centre has been opened at Livingston in Scotland, by the Petroleum Industry Training Board, with the Offshore Petroleum Training Association. It undertakes basic rig crew training for both exploration and production.

But the oil industry is largely dependent on the recruitment of large numbers of technical, scientific and administration personnel. The urgent need is for young, well qualified engineers in all branches, particularly chemical, mechanical and electrical.

Applicants should have a desire to get ahead, for the oil industry is a dynamic and forceful industry which relies on trained personnel with initiative and drive, with ambition, with qualities of leadership and a deep sense of responsibility.

Sixth formers interested in a career in the industry should choose subjects like maths, chemistry and physics for A levels. This will give a choice of most engineering disciplines as well as geology and geophysics for a degree course.

Drillers, tool pushers and drilling superintendents may have begun their career further down the ladder. But along the way they have been to university or technical college as well as on company courses. Never forget that all this study and work – and to reach the top will take at least ten years – is worthwhile. In case you are worried about redundancy when the North Sea fields run dry, it should be stressed that the oil industry is worldwide and there is always work. In fact you will be expected to move around the world by the oil company, usually serving in one location for a period of two to three years.

Specialist courses

Most universities run degree courses in geology, geophysics, engineering, maths and physics. But after obtaining a degree, a graduate must be prepared for further specialized training in subjects such as petroleum engineering.

As Scotland is the major base for oil companies operating in the North Sea, it is logical that the most advanced courses are based there. For example, Heriot Watt University, Edinburgh has a one-year petroleum engineering course which gives honours engineering graduates an understanding and knowledge of the oil industry. For details write to:–

Institute of Offshore Engineering
Heriot Watt University
Research Park
Riccarton
Currie
Edinburgh EH14 4AS

Aberdeen University has a one-year post-graduate geology course which is open to people with 1st or 2nd class honours degree in engineering, maths, physics, geology or geophysics. In the oil industry a poor degree is a poor recommendation for a job.

One-year diploma courses on offshore engineering are provided at Robert Gordon's Institute of Technology. Write to:–

Robert Gordon's Institute of Technology
School of Mechanical and Offshore Engineering
Schoolhill
Aberdeen AB9 1FR.

The Scottish Offshore Training Association, with a membership of more than 50 oil companies, is responsible for training in fire fighting, crane operations, helicopter evacuation, and survival as well as exploration and production accounting. For details write to:–

Scottish Offshore Training Association
Seaforth Centre
Waterloo Quay
Aberdeen AB2 1BS

Divers

For divers, the Underwater Training Centre at Loch Linnhe, runs two basic courses. For details write to:–

The Underwater Training Centre
Inverlochie
Fort William
Inverness

Two other centres, Fort Bovis and Underwater Centre, Plymouth, and Prodive Ltd., Falmouth, Cornwall, have had their training programmes approved for issuing certificates to trainee divers.

Other useful addresses:

Institute of Petroleum
61 New Cavendish Street
London W1M 8AR

Institute of Marine Engineers
76 Mark Lane
London EC3R 7JN

Society for Underwater Technology
1 Birdcage Walk
London SW1H 9JJ

Underwater Engineering Group
6 Storey's Gate
London SW1P 3AU

Careers literature

But whatever you decide you want to do, do check up on the qualifications required first, while you still have time to choose what subjects to study at O- or A-level. The best place for this kind of information is the Petroleum Industry Training Board. The Board has just completed, with the Institute of Petroleum, an up-to-date booklet on "A Career in Oil". Write to:—

The Project Manager
New Entrants and Research
Petroleum Industry Training
  Board
Kingfisher House,
Walton St., Aylesbury,
Buckinghamshire HP21 7TQ.

Books

The majority of books about the oil industry are highly technical. But the Educational or Public Affairs Departments of oil companies or institutions will guide you through them and give helpful advice. They themselves produce a number of free booklets and illustrated pamphlets on various aspects of the oil industry. Write to the Public Relations Officers or Education Officers.

Some of the books mentioned below are rather expensive so you may prefer to look for them in your local library.

The Oil Rush by Mervyn Jones (Quartet Books). A well illustrated paperback giving a description of drilling and exploration and production, and the work involved. It also discusses the impact of oil on Scotland.

Commercial Oil-Field Diving by Nichola B. Zinkowski (Cornell Maritime Press, Cambridge, Maryland, USA). A most readable and well informed book on diving written by a diver.

Oil by Christopher Tugendhat and Adrian Hamilton (Eyre Methuen). An admirable history of recent oil exploration and the politics of the international industry.

The Seven Sisters by Anthony Sampson (Hodder & Stoughton). A study of the seven major oil companies in the international scene, set against the background of the whole industry.

Our Island's Oil by Martin Lovegrove (Witherby & Co.). An excellent study by a geologist who is also deeply involved in analysis of the North Sea fields.

Benefits of North Sea Oil (Scottish Information Office, New St. Andrew's House, Edinburgh EH1 3TD). Free.

Facts about Oil a glossary of terms in the oil and gas industry. (Bank of Scotland Information Service, Oil Division, 38 St. Andrew's Square, Edinburgh EH2 2YR). Free.

A Fact Sheet on oil from the UK Continental Shelf is published at intervals by the Department of Energy. Write to:—

The Library,
The Department of Energy
Thames House South,
Millbank, London, SW1P 4QJ.

Other pamphlets about the oil industry can also be obtained from the Institute of Petroleum.

Films

Most of the big companies have some excellent modern films which they loan out on request. Write to the Publicity Officers of the following:—

British Petroleum
Britannic House, Moor Lane
London, EC2Y 9BU

Shell International
Shell Centre
London, SE1 7NA

Phillips Petroleum (Europe Africa)
Portland House, Stag Place
London SW1E 5DA

Acknowledgments

Key to the position of the illustrations: (T) top; (C) centre; (B) bottom; and combinations, for example: (TR) top right, or (CL) centre left.

Artists
Terry Allen Designs Ltd: 16–17, 20, 22
Hayward Art Group: 5, 13, 14–15, 19, 36, 38, 42–3
Eric Jewell: 6–7, 34–5, 40–41
John Marshall/Temple Art: 22, 28–9
Tony Payne: 4, 10, 31
John Young/Temple Art: 24

Photographs
British Petroleum Company Ltd: jacket (back), 7, 11(BL), 13(B), 15, 25(C), 26, 27(TC) (BL) (BR), 29(R), 30(T), 38, 39(TL) (TR), 41(R), 44
Texaco: jacket (front), 17
Japan Petroleum Development Corporation: 16
Whittaker Survival Systems Capsule: 30(T)
Compagnie Française des Pétroles-Total: 9(T), 12, 27(TL), 31, 33(T)
Bernsen's International Press Service Ltd: 32
Mobil: 33(B), 18(B), 27(TR)
Seaphot: 2, 21(TL) (BL) (R), 22, 46
Shell International Petroleum Company Ltd: 8(T) (B), 11(BR), 13(T), 19(T), 37(TL) (CL) (TR), 43(T)
Esso Petroleum Company Ltd: 9(B), 11(TR)
Conoco: 11(TL)
Fay Godwin: 24
Exxon Corporation: 25(B)
Vautier-Decool: 25(T)
Phillips Norway Group: 41(TL)
IHC, Holland: 41(BL)
Neste Oy, Helsinki: 43(B)
Royal Society for the Protection of Birds: 5(TR)
Central Press Photos Ltd: 5(B)
Abu Dhabi Petroleum Company Ltd: 37(BL)
Santa Fé International Corporation: 45
Snamprogetti, Milan: 37 (BR)
Vautier-de Nanxe: 39(BL) (BR)

Index